D1766031

Mapping Global Racisms

Series Editor
Ian Law
School of Sociology and Social Policy
University of Leeds
Leeds, UK

There is no systematic coverage of the racialisation of the planet. This series is the first attempt to present a comprehensive mapping of global racisms, providing a way in which to understand global racialisation and acknowledge the multiple generations of different racial logics across regimes and regions. Unique in its intellectual agenda and innovative in producing a new empirically-based theoretical framework for understanding this glocalised phenomenon, Mapping Global Racisms considers racism in many underexplored regions such as Russia, Arab racisms in North African and Middle Eastern contexts, and racism in Pacific contries such as Japan, Hawaii, Fiji and Samoa.

More information about this series at
http://www.palgrave.com/gp/series/14813

Katy P. Sian

Navigating Institutional Racism in British Universities

Katy P. Sian
Department of Sociology
University of York
York, UK

Mapping Global Racisms
ISBN 978-3-030-14283-4   ISBN 978-3-030-14284-1   (eBook)
https://doi.org/10.1007/978-3-030-14284-1

Cover image: © Pete Lusabia/Alamy Stock Photo

This Palgrave Macmillan imprint is published by the registered company Springer Nature Switzerland AG
The registered company address is: Gewerbestrasse 11, 6330 Cham, Switzerland

*In loving memory of my grandfather Sohan Singh Loyal,
and my uncle Balvinder Singh Loyal.*

Acknowledgements

Friedrich Nietzsche said that a good writer possesses not only their own spirit, but also the spirit of their friends.[1] With this in mind, I would first of all like to thank all of the wonderful participants for taking the time to be involved within the conversations that make the backbone of this book. Thank you for sharing your lived experiences, critical insights and personal reflections, all of which have made this text come to life. I would like to thank my family and loved ones for their constant support and strength throughout the writing of this book; thanks to Lucinda and Sarah, and of course Karandeep for your unwavering patience and positivity. Mum, my voice always seeks to channel your resilience; your journey, your fight and your resistance continues to inspire me. You are the strongest woman I know, and I want to thank you for building up my courage and never allowing me to give up in the face of exclusionary structures of racism. Thank you for empowering me.

A special thanks to those friends and colleagues who have continued to stand by my side; I am deeply grateful for these connections and the ongoing encouragement and guidance that I am blessed to receive. In particular, Rita Kaur Dhamoon, Richard Burgon, Roshni Narian, Fairn Herising, Dave Beer, S. Sayyid, Raven Bowen, Wes Lin, Marta Araújo,

R. Sabir, Shirley Anne Tate, and Kwame Nimako. I would especially like to mention Silvia Rodríguez Maseo, María Martínez, and Gabriel Gatti, who supported and published the paper that would come to be the foundation of this book, 'Being Black in a White World: Understanding Racism in British universities' *International Journal on Collective Identity Research*, Vol. 176, No. 2, 2017, 1–26. Thanks also to David Gillborn and Kalwant Bhopal for inviting me to share some of the ideas expressed in this book at the 2018 CREE conference on 'Race and Education in the Trump/Brexit era,' Birmingham.

A heartfelt thanks to Ian Law for having faith in this project and for supporting me throughout the years. Finally thanks to the excellent editorial and production teams at Palgrave, and also the reviewers who have helped with the completion of this publication.

Note

1. Nietzsche, F. (1996). *Human, All Too Human: A Book for Free Spirits* (R. J. Hollingdale, Trans.) (p. 9), Cambridge: Cambridge University Press.

Praise for *Navigating Institutional Racism in British Universities*

"In this groundbreaking and thought provoking book, Katy Sian explores and examines the persistence of racism in British universities. She carefully documents the realities of daily life for black and minority ethnic academics working in higher education. Offering a set of important recommendations, this book is crucial for those interested in challenging discriminatory cultures. A timely and courageous intervention."
—Richard Burgon MP, *Member of Parliament for Leeds East, Shadow Secretary of State for Justice and Shadow Lord Chancellor, UK*

"In the wake of student cries to decolonise and the scandal of endemic racism in higher education, there can be no better time for Katy Sian's powerful forensic analysis to enter the stage, bringing clarity, wisdom and hope to the many people of colour who strive to survive *in the heart of whiteness* that is the British academy."
—Heidi Safia Mirza, *Professor of Race, Faith and Culture at Goldsmiths, University of London, UK. Co-editor* Dismantling Race in Higher Education: Racism, Whiteness and Decolonising the Academy

"White supremacy finds expression in multiple ways; sometimes it screams from the barrel of a gun, at other times it operates through the hidden business-as-usual routines of everyday life that constantly exclude, oppress, belittle and do violence to people of colour. Sian's book fearlessly documents and challenges the racism that lies at the heart of British universities. This is a passionate, complex, and conceptually nuanced book that exposes the multiple ways in which racism defines higher education and offers practical steps in shaping the changes that must happen."
—David Gillborn, *Director of the Centre for Research in Race & Education, University of Birmingham, UK. Editor of* 'Race Ethnicity and Education'

"This is an outstanding book which resonates with my own survival in the academy. Katy Sian brilliantly excavates and exposes the hidden operations of racism through Critical Race Theory story-telling of racially marked academics and the epistemic violence they endure on a daily basis. This book is essential reading for White senior and middle leaders in British universities. The question remains, will they read it and act to change practice within their own university?"
—Vini Lander, *Professor of Race and Teacher Education, University of Roehampton, UK*

Contents

1

Introduction

Debunking the 'Liberal' University

This book has been a long time coming. If we start the story from my PhD, I have been in the academy for around twelve years. This, I believe, is a sufficient amount of time to deliver a 'longitudinal' piece of ethnography that is reflexive and most of all candid and critical. Let me begin with a few disclaimers. This is not a book that has been interfered with, or shaped by, a clinical, soulless, REF criterion.[1] The 'originality,' 'significance,' and 'rigour' of the text to follow, is not for a small group of white professors—sitting on a research committee—to deliberate or determine. These folks are likely to be ill-equipped to deal with the issues raised by this book, for it requires them to confront their own histories and current practices. In that sense, this piece of research is most definitely not concerned with striving for a 'high star rating' that will go onto contribute to detached, neoliberal university league tables.

This book isn't written by an 'angry' woman of colour; it isn't anti-white, nor is it simply seeking to be 'reactive' or 'polemical.' As a female academic of colour who is perhaps able to 'pass' racial lines more easily than others (superficially, rather than structurally), who isn't deemed too

© The Author(s) 2019
K. P. Sian, *Navigating Institutional Racism in British Universities*,
Mapping Global Racisms, https://doi.org/10.1007/978-3-030-14284-1_1

'ethnic,' and who holds a degree of job stability, I am writing this book because I realize that I am perhaps in a slightly better position to do so than some of my peers. It arises from years of observation, on-going conversations with academic friends from across the globe, and the development of a voice that hopes to be fearless and in keeping with the spirit of the invaluable mentoring I received, and continue to receive, from an academic of colour. The book might be best read as a collectively driven piece of work. It seeks to centre the voices of my respondents and creatively engage with their journeys as well as my own, taking seriously the anger, the tears, the laughter and most of all the strategies adopted to challenge the white academy. It is a book for all those who want to actively, and profoundly think about how we might transform the university both structurally and conceptually. This is not an exhaustive rant, nor a story of victimhood. This is a narrative of survival and resistance in a space that continues to exclude, devalue and dismiss our *being*.

Racism is the dirty secret hiding behind a string of superficial tag lines that have come to brand universities across the UK. The following myths about the 'liberal' university can often be seen touted in marketing brochures, job announcements and website pages promoting the values and responsibilities of the institution:

Myth 1: Universities encourage inclusivity and diversity
Myth 2: Universities invest in racially marked academics
Myth 3: Universities are 'post-racial'
Myth 4: Universities desire curriculum reform
Myth 5: Universities are committed to race equality

Beyond these false advertising scams, the real message is clear and simple: Racism in British universities is endemic. This is not 'hot off the press.' Academic research has pointed to this fact for well over 20 years.[2] Alongside the research, there is also a catalogue of data that explicitly shows the bleak prospects for racially marked academics. To understand the longevity of institutional racism within British universities, one must interrogate its racial history, its white supremacist politics, and its patterns of privilege. Whiteness is a system of violence. The university is structured by whiteness. It follows then, that the university is both a transmitter and a maintainer of violence. By violence I mean that which is both systemic/structural and epistemic/symbolic. As the book exposes throughout, such articulations of violence interplay and intertwine to produce a series of long-term harms that are legitimized by racist power structures. The failure of senior managers to accept or even acknowledge the existence of systematic racism operating in their universities, departments, faculties, and boardrooms is where the heart of the problem lies. Over decades the default option has been to ignore the issue, meaning that structurally nothing significant has changed. Racism isn't necessarily worse for racially marked academics today; it is as hard now as it was back in the 1950s for racially marked academics to prosper in universities. The climate however has undoubtedly changed creating new pressures and demands making the space more difficult to navigate for those who dare to enter this demanding career.

Aims and Objectives

Informed by a series of in-depth conversations and personal reflections, this book sets out to critically examine the experiences of racism encountered by racially marked academics working within British universities. The text seeks to investigate the various ways in which racism in the academy is performed, maintained and reproduced. Through its rich insights and conceptual enquiry, this book explores both the structural and interpersonal nature of racism enacted in spaces of higher education. It unpacks a range of complex and challenging questions and engages with the way in which racial politics in the university can be seen to intersect with broader issues around gender. The book presents a textured narrative around the key barriers facing racially marked academics, and aims to enhance understandings of institutional racism in British universities. It seeks to develop a series of practical recommendations to encourage and support the participation of racially marked academics in higher education. These issues are of increasing relevance for all those in the sector, particularly in the wake of contemporary global issues such as internationalization, decolonizing the curriculum, and the 'diversity' agenda.

The need for this book is clear. Statistics around Black and Minority Ethnic (BME)[3] representation in universities continue to demonstrate that racially marked academics are marginalized from British universities. Data generated from the Higher Education Statistics Agency (HESA) in 2012/2013 revealed that out of 17,880 professors, only 85 were Black, 950 were Asian, 365 were 'other' (including mixed), while the majority 15,200 were White (Bhopal 2015: Runnymede Trust). In terms of black female professors there are just 17 in the entire British university system (Runnymede Trust: 2015), and in January 2017 the *Guardian* newspaper reported that for the third year in a row, HESA figures recorded no black academics in the elite staff category of managers, directors and senior officials in 2015/2016 (Adams 2017: Guardian). Alongside the data there is also extensive literature documenting on-going practices of institutional racism in universities, including the gutting of race equality policy, limited access to career advancement, fewer opportunities for promotion, and daily experiences of discrimination (Sian 2017: 1–26). The persistence of racism in British universities shows that at the top very little has been done to encourage progress and racial equality.

Book Outline

Chapter 2 will provide some reflections on method. It will map out the broader conceptual approach, which is informed by critical race theory and black/postcolonial feminism. Such frameworks will enable readers to understand both the lived experiences and the structural dimensions of power operating within British universities. These tools allow for key insights into the ways in which university spaces are structured and patterned by racism. As a female academic of colour, I will also engage with auto-ethnography to allow my own reflections to run throughout the text.

My conversations with racially marked academics unravelled the complex interplay between microaggressions and practices of institutional racism. All of my respondents opened their interviews by detailing a series of incidents related to their day-to-day experiences in their departments as a way to set the scene about the space that they inhabit. Chapter 3 will thus focus on the performance of these everyday exclusionary interactions and examine how they operate to reinforce structures of whiteness in the academy. The chapter will draw upon issues concerning subtle forms of racism—or liberal racism, feelings of isolation, 'otherness,' and hyper-visibility and invisibility. In this chapter, the resemblance across the responses will be highlighted as a way to point to the widespread nature of institutional racism. It will uncover the ways in which covert, structural processes of racism—both implicitly and explicitly—maintain systems of whiteness at the expense of racialized bodies; who are positioned as outsiders.

The classroom is often thought to represent a 'safe space' that promotes critical learning, the exchange of ideas, and pedagogical tools to generate future knowledge. However, the university classroom is not free from racial (and gendered) politics, therefore for many racially marked academics, the classroom is also the site in which students express feelings of white resentment, white guilt and white privilege. My data demonstrates the challenges that racially marked academics encounter when teaching including, having their authority undermined, feeling ridiculed, and often being fearful to teach the next class. Chapter 4 will as such draw upon the emotional and psychological strains of teaching within British universities, and explore how racially marked academics have attempted to navigate this complex space.

Interrupting hegemonic forms of knowledge in British universities requires a deep sense of structural transformation. The social sciences curriculum in particular, is central in reproducing Eurocentric knowledge arising from the European colonial enterprise. This knowledge is problematic as it is based upon a narrow set of ideas, racial classifications, and 'universal truths' to maintain a distinction between the 'modern' and 'civilized' West, and the 'primitive' 'uncivilized' Non-West. Calls to critically challenge the reproduction of these knowledges form the basis for the movement to decolonize the curriculum. Chapter 5 sets out to examine the difficulties that my respondents have faced in their attempts to unsettle conventional social science curricula. It will also demonstrate the importance of creating new epistemological spaces in enabling educators and students to engage with 'other' knowledges and situate global issues in nuanced frameworks.

British universities have ensured that a range of diversity and equality policies have been generated to promote positive action and inclusion. However, despite these strategies, my respondents consistently documented experiences of being unsupported, undervalued, and their contributions being dismissed. All my respondents expressed feelings of instability in the academy with very little guidance and reassurance from senior members of staff. Chapter 6 will address issues around lack of mentorship, insecurities around job stability, and barriers to career progression.

Chapter 7 will explore the various strategies of resistance that my respondents have developed as a way to navigate, resist, and survive racism in university spaces. It will provide a detailed exploration of the various mechanisms that they have adopted to deal with racism, and also discuss the importance of, and challenges around, developing wider networks to ensure support and solidarity. The chapter will examine the different channels available for racially marked academics and the activity that has already taken place to successfully manage, and cope with, challenging environments that are structured by institutional racism.

Chapter 8 will set out a series of recommendations for policy and practice in British universities around how to challenge racism effectively. It will discuss the importance of providing clear access to paths for progression to ensure that racially marked academics can fully participate within the sector. It will propose that in order to understand the root causes of the persistent position of disadvantage experienced by racially marked academics, a conceptual and proactive dialogue is required around institutional racism, Eurocentric knowledge production, and the destabilizing of whiteness. The book concludes by reflecting upon how we might transform the structures of racism inherent within British universities, and indeed if such transformation is even possible.

Notes

1. REF refers to the 'Research Excellence Framework.' It is a system for 'evaluating' the quality of research across universities in the UK.
2. For example of such literature, see: Neal, S. (1998) *The Making of Equal Opportunities Policies in Universities*, Buckingham: Open University Press; Modood, T., and Ackland, T. (1998) *Race and Higher Education*, London: Policy Studies Institute; Gillborn, D. (1995) *Racism and Antiracism in Real Schools: Theory, Policy, Practice*, Buckingham: Open University Press; Mirza, H. (1992) *Young, Female and Black*, London: Routledge; Bhopal, K. (1994) 'The Influence of Feminism on Black Women in the Higher Education Curriculum,' in Davies, S., Lubelska, C., and Quinn, J. (Eds.) *Changing the Subject: Women in Higher Education*, pp. 124–137, London: Taylor and Francis.
3. The term 'BME' refers to a category that emerged in the UK to classify ethnically marked populations that were distinct from the idea of the white European national majority. Prior to the BME classification, ethnically marked populations were grouped as 'coloured' and then 'black' (Cumberbatch 2009: 160). There is a debate around how such collective terms exclude and include various population groups. BME, like BAME (Black And Minority Ethnic), BOEM (Black and Other Ethnic Minority), or BEM (Black and Ethnic Minority)—and other classifications—are contested concepts and are likely to remain so in a racialized environment such as that of Britain. In this book, the use of the term BME is pragmatic rather than devotional.

References

Adams, R. (2017, January 19). *British Universities Employ No Black Academics in Top Roles, Figures Show*. London: Guardian. https://www.theguardian.com/education/2017/jan/19/british-universities-employ-no-black-academics-in-top-roles-figures-show.
Bhopal, K. (2015, July 17). *The Experiences of Black and Minority Ethnic Academics*. London: Runnymede Trust. https://www.runnymedetrust.org/blog/the-experiences-of-black-and-minority-ethnic-academics.
Cumberbatch, M. (2009). Multiculturalism Is an Essential Part of the Anti-racist Struggle. In A. Pilkington, S. Housee, & K. Hylton (Eds.), *Race(ing)*

Forward: Transitions in Theorising 'Race' in Education (pp. 149–166). Birmingham: Centre for Sociology, Anthropology and Politics (C-SAP), Higher Education Academy.

Runnymede Trust. (2015). *Black Students Must Do Better Than White Students to Get into University*. London: Runnymede Trust. https://www.runnymedetrust.org/news/594/272/Black-Students-Must-do-Better-than-White-Students-to-get-into-University.html.

Sian, K. (2017). Being Black in a White World: Understanding Racism in British Universities. *International Journal on Collective Identity Research, 176*(2), 1–26.

2

A Brief Reflection on Methods and Conceptual Framings

Research Method

This book is a collection of different voices who have shared with me their pain, their strength, their challenges, their courage, and their resistance to racism in the academy. For years I have found myself engaged in the same conversation with academics of colour, from all over the globe, always prompted by the question, 'so how is work?' The familiar response is that of an eye roll, followed by a sigh, and even a slight laugh, alerting the other to what we already know, what we already feel, and what we are already experiencing in our own university. And just like that we share; we share the all too recognizable stories, the frustrations, the relief that we are not alone, paranoid, or being unreasonable. We listen, we laugh, and we see in each other's eyes that we are together in our struggle. We smile, because in that moment we feel stronger, and grateful that we have had the space be heard. I am thankful to my academic friends of colour who over the years have listened to me, allowed me to share, and provided me with the strength and support that I would have never had gotten elsewhere.

© The Author(s) 2019
K. P. Sian, *Navigating Institutional Racism in British Universities*,
Mapping Global Racisms, https://doi.org/10.1007/978-3-030-14284-1_2

These conversations equipped me mentally, they prepared me practically, and in doing so they helped me to survive my workplace. As I
continued in my academic career, I soon got to thinking what about
all those who are unable to share, who haven't had the luxury of having
others to speak too, who have felt alone, excluded and isolated? And
so the foundations of the book began, as I sought to speak with those
who hadn't had the opportunity to fully communicate the depth and
complexity of their answer to the question, 'so how is work?' My interviews, or conversations as I prefer, were with academics of colour and of
difference, all at various stages in their careers. Academics of difference
refer to those who may be considered in their own nations as white,
however, are unable to make this white privilege travel to a post-Brexit
Britain. As a result, they begin to experience degrees of racialization that
ethnically mark them as subaltern (Hesse and Sayyid 2006: 21–24).
However, there is also recognition that although they may be subjected
to particular forms of exclusion, academics of difference still maintain
a much greater degree of privilege compared to academics of colour.
That is, academics of difference are far more able to mobilize and call
upon a set of cultural resources that remain unavailable to academics of
colour.

Due to the variation of my respondents, we can see the way in which
'differential racialization' both develops and unfolds (Chan et al. 2014:
4–5). The book is therefore cognizant of the diverse racial histories that
my respondents occupy, and makes no attempt to homogenize or gen-
eralize their experiences, but rather seeks to critically explore how they
differ, overlap, and intersect with other categories of oppression against
the landscape of the white academy. The respondents will thus be
referred to as *racially marked academics*, as a way to capture the diverse
experiences through which practices of racial 'othering' take place. We
will see the complex ways in which cultural, ethnic, religious, and phenotypical identifications interconnect in the marking out, or racialization, of those considered 'outside' dominant forms of whiteness (Moore
2003: 273–274; Meer and Modood 2010: 77; Sian 2017: 40). Through
these varied patterns of racialization, we will also uncover the ways in
which race-making processes inform, shape, and impact wider exclusionary social relations in the academy.

When our conversations opened, that same eye roll, that same sigh, and that same uncomfortable laugh, was to be seen and heard, signalling immediately that one familiar feeling, exhaustion. Whether in my office, in their office, or in a coffee shop the conversations flowed. For some, it was like they had needed the space to finally get things off their chest, a therapy session, where they could speak about their experiences in the academy. As various encounters were shared, there were tears, sometimes from them, and at other times from me. There was laughter, there was anger, and there was pain. Undeniably, there was also a sense of defiance, perseverance, and resistance. Some conversations were particularly emotional and harder than others. On some occasions, hours and even days after they had taken place, I found myself replaying their experiences in my head overcome with a deep feeling of sadness that our bodies had all been injured in someway or another by systemic, structural, and symbolic manifestations of racism in our universities.

As I write these words I receive a text message from a close friend, who is an academic of colour working outside the UK. Disturbed and angry she details an incident in which she had to call out her white colleague's blatant racism, which left her feeling anxious. We dissect the encounter, I give her the space to unload and then offer reassurance. As we exit the conversation she thanks me and writes, 'I needed not to be alone with it.' At this point it couldn't be clearer to me that the act of sharing these all too frequent occurrences is significant both for our healing and our recovery. It also works as an important reminder that these conversations, both formal and informal, are disturbingly commonplace. It alerts me to all the energy and labour that we have to invest in order to manage and minimize the physical and psychological harm that these incidents so often provoke.

The experiences documented throughout this book sit alongside snippets of my own personal encounters, to form what might be described as a map for others to use to help them to navigate their own clashes with racism in the university. I hope to take away that sense of isolation and exclusion that we, as racially marked academics, so often feel, by demonstrating that we are in it together, and that we are not alone in the racism that we experience on a daily basis in our white institutions. I had 20 conversations in total. I spoke with a fairly equal mix of male and female respondents, ranging from early career, mid-career, and advanced career academics, working either as lecturers or researchers, on permanent, part-time or fixed-term contracts. They come from a range of racial, ethnonational, and religious groups and are based at Russell Group and Post-1992 universities across Britain,[1] broadly located within the social sciences and humanities disciplines. The book is organized around key themes arising from the conversations, based upon microaggressions and day-to-day office politics; teaching and decolonizing the curriculum; promotions and career advancement; and resistance. This piece should therefore be read as a collective body of work, where our voices have come together to reveal our shared struggles in the white academy.

I don't wish to get too distracted here by detached methodological concerns around sampling, objectivity, validity and so on. The statistical data on under-representation already does a stellar job of 'quantifying' racism in the academy, my participants and their experiences therefore need not be subjected to classification or measurability, for this is a text of rich documentation in which the 'evidence' speaks lucidly for itself. Through what is typically described as critical (auto)ethnography, the text to follow makes no attempt for claims of universality or scientific 'truths,' but rather it seeks to present the persistent and widespread nature of racism in British universities, by demonstrating both its everydayness and structural nature. That is, I am primarily focused on understanding how experiences are signified, constructed and represented within institutional cultures (Hall 1992: 290–292; Sayyid and Zac 1998: 249–268). My reluctance around detailing a grand methodological design is twofold. First it expects me to provide information that I am unwilling to share, in particular, regarding the specificities of my sample. The requirement to do so in order to prove 'rigour' is symptomatic of broader, problematic procedures inherent within the social sciences that are unable to understand or respect the real anxieties that people of colour encounter as a result of participating within such research. This leads to the second point which is that which refuses to reproduce, or worse, celebrate, a narrow, European, empirical framework that is assumed to be the only legitimate way to conduct meaningful research.

Such refusal might be loosely described as partaking within the project to decolonize methodologies, which would certainly be in keeping with the overall tone of the book. That is, this research actively steps out of essentializing, Eurocentric discourses. It takes the shared experiences, narratives and voices seriously by centring, rather than marginalizing, their textured accounts. As Hartej Gill, Kadi Purru, and Gloria Lin point out, adopting a decolonial research framework allows us to, 'claim, reclaim, support and legitimize "other" epistemological positions in the academy' (2012: 11). It is a serious attempt to dismantle the conventional research binary of insiders and outsiders, and uncovers instead, 'a complicated, fluid and messy process rather than a clearly defined methodology' (ibid.). A decolonial posturing, as Goodwin Y. Agboka describes, 'is an invitation to deconstruct Western-influenced research traditions and essentialist perspectives through collaborations between researchers and non researchers' (2014: 303). This book thus situates itself within the spirit of a decolonial methodological approach, which arises from a close engagement with the data to develop an analytical critique of praxis associated with coloniality and racism.

Conceptual Tools

The conceptual frameworks that this book aligns itself with are critical race theory (CRT) and black/postcolonial feminism. CRT and black/postcolonial feminism enable rich insights into understanding the complex ways in which performance and practice are both enacted and conditioned by structures of race and gender (Chan et al. 2014: 4–7). Combined they allow me to examine the ways in which lived experiences interplay with wider structural dimensions of power operating within universities. Both are instruments that facilitate social justice for racially marked groups (ibid.). CRT emerged during the 1970s in the US as a response to the 'rolling back' of the advances made by the 1960s Civil Rights Movement (Delgado and Stefancic 1993: 461). It sought to critically address the multifaceted relationship between race, racism, and the law, by deploying new theories and ideas to capture this complexity (ibid.). CRT initially developed as a critique of law

(Chan et al. 2014: 4), as a means to uncover the ways in which legal discourse has been embedded and reproduced to legitimize, and support racist power structures (Crenshaw 1988: 1350). It has since expanded its scope, shifting from legal scholarship to encompass and address the historic, systemic, and routinized configurations of racism. Thandeka Chapman and Jamel Donnor point to the way in which, as a conceptual lens CRT, 'provides a legal, historicized framework for explicating and analyzing how policies and institutionalized practices reinforce inequities' (2015: 138), that is, it links the historical production of race and racism to contemporary exercises of marginalization, oppression, and subordination in organized and everyday settings (ibid.). In doing so it enables us to both recognize and identify the intricate ways in which race has manifested itself within systems and structures to reenact discourses of white supremacy.

In this sense CRT refers to a framework that attempts to broadly, 'critique social reality and the dynamics of power between race discourse and institutions, bodies, and subjectivity, specifically to reveal that racism is ordinary and normalized' (Chan et al. 2014: 4). The normalization, the ordinariness, and the 'everydayness' of racism (Essed 1991), is of particular interest for those of us engaged with CRT, as it allows for an analysis which treats racism as 'not aberrant' (Delgado 1995: xiv), but rather as that which is sewn into the very tapestry of Western societies, in other words, CRT compels us to understand that racism is 'enmeshed in the fabric of our social order, it appears both normal and natural to people in this culture' (Ladson-Billings 1998: 11). David Gillborn argues that CRT thus recognizes that racism is not only that which refers to overt forms of racial hatred, but also that which relates to hidden practices of power that disadvantage racially marked communities (2006: 22). CRT is therefore a project that directly challenges liberal conceptions of racism, which tend to mask its structural and systemic nature. Through the centering of racism, CRT calls for a rich, scholarly analysis that is 'engaged in the process of rejecting and deconstructing the current patterns of exclusion and oppression' (ibid.: 27). Related to this, a key element of CRT is the notion of *interest convergence*, which alerts us to the way in which racism advances the privileges and benefits of the white establishment (Bell 1980), racism thus becomes a tool that is mobilized by white elites to serve their own interests.

Interwoven with the decolonial methodological framework as outlined in the previous section, an important practical component of CRT is that which recognizes the strength of storytelling (Ladson-Billings 1998: 8). Storytelling is an essential feature of CRT as it helps us, 'to build a powerful challenge to "mainstream" assumptions' (Gillborn 2006: 24). As Gillborn goes onto describe, such an approach allows us to understand and reflect upon, 'the importance of context and the detail of the lived experience of minoritized peoples as a defence against the colour-blind and sanitized analyses generated via universalistic discourses' (ibid.: 23). It provides racially marked communities with a critical space to write our own narratives, open up new questions, and unsettle essentializing discourses. Storytelling in this sense becomes not only a creative art form, but also a valuable political tool that speaks back at, challenges, and resists oppressive structures of whiteness. CRT has clear significance and relevance for this book. Through its analytical understandings and rich insights, CRT enables me to craft a reflective yet elucidative account of racism in British universities, directly informed by my own experiences, as well as those of my participants. At the heart of this book is a story of racism, and CRT allows me to unapologetically develop this as the focal point, it does not force or compel me to bring in a series of other 'social indicators' that will detract from its centrality. The story to follow is one that not only takes seriously the normalization of racism in universities, but also recognizes at the same time how its normalization is bound up and interconnected with the wider workings of (white) structural power. It challenges liberal notions of racism that are entrenched within the university setting, and critiques processes and practices that continue to privilege whiteness at the expense of racially marked bodies. Through its complexities, its nuances, and its potential to disrupt, CRT has been the only home from which I desire to write and tell this story.

The book also engages with broader elements of black/postcolonial feminist thought, which connects with CRT to furnish a language of resistance, solidarity, and liberation, as Heidi Mirza argues, 'the contingent and critical project of black and postcolonial feminisms is to chart

the story of raced and gendered domination across different landscapes'
(2009: 2). Black/postcolonial feminism is drawn upon to unravel the
patterning of gendered racism, as a way to understand the racial oppression and exclusion experienced by my respondents as that which is,
'structured by racist and ethnicist perceptions of gender roles' (Essed
1991: 31). In doing so, we are able to illuminate the practices by which
both racially marked women and men are disciplined and marginalized
through racist, essentialist discourses, that replay and reaffirm earlier
reductive, white supremacist, classifications. The book thus takes into
account that while the racism manifests itself differently upon female
and male racially marked bodies, it nonetheless remains organized by
racist constructions of gender roles (e.g. 'passive brown woman'; 'black
male rapist,' etc.) (ibid.). By carefully considering the different ways
in which race and gender interplay and interact, we are able to identify how multiple oppressions are layered upon bodies of difference,
to further restrict and prevent their participation and advancement in
university spaces, that assume hegemonic forms of whiteness, maleness,
heterosexuality, and ableism.

In taking the lived, embodied experience as politically relevant,
black/postcolonial feminism allows us to understand the varied ways in
which difference is inscribed upon the racially marked body, and identify how those etchings unfold through practices of exclusion (Ahmed
2004: 117–139). By situating my experiences alongside those of my
respondents, I am, to quote Patricia Hill-Collins, 'one voice in a dialogue among people who have been silenced' (2002: ix). This has enabled for the development of a community of voices that are deeply
involved within a collective critique of racism in British universities.
We are therefore, 'engaged in the process of quilting a genealogical narrative of "other ways of knowing"' (Mirza 2009: 2). These 'other ways
of knowing' become important sites of resistance, empowerment and
intervention. By focusing on what Mirza describes as 'embodied difference' the book addresses the complex processes of 'being and becoming a gendered and raced subject' (ibid.). Documenting the experiences
in such a way thus allows for agency and representation, whereby the
interactions, interfaces, and intersubjectivities become a central, rather
than a marginal, feature of the book.

Combined then, CRT and black/postcolonial feminism provide valuable, analytical tools for both imagining and reimagining the destabilization of racialized and gendered systems of oppression that currently exist in the British university. The methodological and conceptual frameworks of this book can therefore be seen as those that situate themselves as an attempt to interlink a set of theoretical and practical questions. The story to follow is concerned with understanding the structural and symbolic patternings of racism in higher education, as well as revealing the way in which racism is embodied, internalized and resisted in the performances of racially marked academics. That is, conceptually and methodologically, this account recognizes the agency of those of us involved in this dialogue, and with that agency, it opens up the prospect of imagining an anti-racist university.

Note

1. The Russell Group represents 24 UK universities. These are often considered to be "elite" institutions that have a reputation for academic excellence and producing highly rated research. Post-1992 universities refer to previous tertiary education teaching institutions (polytechnics) that were granted university status under the Further and Higher Education Act 1992.

References

Agboka, G. (2014). Decolonial Methodologies: Social Justice Perspectives in Intercultural Technical Communication Research. *Journal of Technical Writing and Communication, 44*(3), 297–327.

Ahmed, S. (2004). Affective Economies. *Social Text, 79, 22*(2), 117–139.

Bell, D. (1980). Brown v. Board of Education and the Interest Convergence Dilemma. *Harvard Law Review, 93*(3), 518–533.

Chan, A., Dhamoon, R., & Moy, L. (2014). Metaphoric Representations of Women of Colour in the Academy: Teaching Race, Disrupting Power. *Borderlands, 13*(2), 1–26.

Chapman, T., & Donnor, J. (2015). Critical Race Theory and the Proliferation of U.S. Charter Schools. *Equity & Excellence in Education, 48*(1), 137–157.

Crenshaw, K. (1988). Race, Reform, Retrenchment: Transformation and Legitimation in Anti-discrimination Law. *Harvard Law Review, 101*(7), 1331–1387.

Delgado, R. (Ed.). (1995). *Critical Race Theory: The Cutting Edge.* Philadelphia: Temple University Press.

Delgado, R., & Stefancic, J. (1993). Critical Race Theory: An Annotated Bibliography. *Virginia Law Review, 79*(2), 461–516.

Essed, P. (1991). *Understanding Everyday Racism: An Interdisciplinary Theory.* Newbury Park: Sage.

Gill, H., Purru, K., & Lin, G. (2012). In the Midst of Participatory Action Research Practices: Moving Towards Decolonizing and Decolonial Praxis. *Reconceptualizing Educational Research Methodology, 3*(1), 1–15.

Gillborn, D. (2006). Critical Race Theory and Education: Racism and Antiracism in Educational Theory and Praxis. *Discourse: Studies in the Cultural Politics of Education, 27*(1), 11–32.

Hall, S. (1992). The West and the Rest: Discourse and Power. In S. Hall & B. Gieben (Eds.), *Formations of Modernity* (pp. 275–332). Cambridge: Polity Press.

Hesse, B., & Sayyid, S. (2006). The Postcolonial Political and the Immigrant Imaginary. In N. Ali, V. Kalra, & S. Sayyid (Eds.), *A Postcolonial People: South Asians in Britain* (pp. 13–31). London: Hurst and Company.

Hill-Collins, P. (2002). *Black Feminist Thought: Knowledge, Consciousness, and the Politics of Empowerment.* New York: Routledge.

Ladson-Billings, G. (1998). Just What Is Critical Race Theory and What's It Doing in a Nice Field Like Education? *International Journal of Qualitative Studies in Education, 11*(1), 7–24.

Meer, N., & Modood, T. (2010). The Racialisation of Muslims. In S. Sayyid & A. Vakil (Eds.), *Thinking Through Islamophobia, Global Perspectives* (pp. 69–83). London: Hurst.

Mirza, H. (2009). Plotting a History: Black and Postcolonial Feminisms in "New Times". *Race Ethnicity and Education, 12*(1), 1–10.

Moore, R. (2003). Racialization. In G. Bolaffi, R. Bracalenti, P. Braham, & S. Gindro (Eds.), *Dictionary of Race, Ethnicity and Culture* (pp. 273–274). London: Sage.

Sayyid, B., & Zac, L. (1998). Political Analysis in a World Without Foundations. In E. Scarbrough & E. Tanenbaum (Eds.), *Research Strategies in the Social Sciences: A Guide to New Approaches* (pp. 249–268). Oxford: Oxford University Press.

Sian, K. (2017). Surveillance, Islamophobia, and Sikh Bodies in the War on Terror. *Islamophobia Studies Journal, 4*(1), 37–52.

3

Microaggressions, Whiteness and the Politics of Exclusion

Introduction

When I think of 'the university,' the image that immediately springs to mind is Jordan Peele's brilliantly chilling film 'Get Out.' When the movie first released I was keen to watch it, and it has stayed on my mind ever since. The film is about a young black male photographer (Chris), who visits his girlfriends white middle-class parents for the weekend. Her parents live in a large house, in white suburbia, occupying acres of land. When they first meet Chris, the dad in particular is keen to demonstrate that he is a good liberal American. He takes Chris on a house tour who immediately notices that both the housekeeper and the gardener are black. The exchange is as follows:

> **Dean Armitage (Father)**: Come on, I get it. White family, black servants. It's a total cliché.
> **Chris Washington**: I wasn't going to take it there.
> **Dean Armitage**: Well you didn't have to, believe me. Now, we hired Georgina and Walter to help care for my parents. When they died I just couldn't bear to let them go. But boy, I hate how it looks.

© The Author(s) 2019
K. P. Sian, *Navigating Institutional Racism in British Universities*,
Mapping Global Racisms, https://doi.org/10.1007/978-3-030-14284-1_3

Chris Washington: Yeah, I know what you mean.
Dean Armitage: By the way, I would have voted for Obama for a third term if I could. Best president in my lifetime. Hands down.[1]

The Obama comment is telling of the post-racial liberal imaginary, which is used in this instance, to over-compensate for the fact that 'the help,' is obviously attached to racial histories rooted in slavery. The over-the-top praise for Obama therefore serves to conveniently dismiss this history and deny its significance or importance. The next day— following a night of Chris being subjected to his girlfriends' mother performing hypnotherapy on him—the parents throw a lavish garden party. Here the parents friends all gather and continue the liberal façade, where they make references to Tiger Woods, and fetishize black culture. Chris's facial expressions immediately signal his sense of discomfort and uneasiness; it is clear that he feels that he does not belong. He is well aware that he is one of only a handful of black people among a sea of wealthy white middle class 'liberals,' in a wealthy white middle-class setting. The guests try to casually show him that they're 'with it' through a string of cringe-worthy gestures. As the story unfolds Chris learns a sinister side to his girlfriend and her family, and as he finds himself trapped he does everything to escape and *get out*.

The triumph of this film lies in the fact that the perpetrators of violent racism are not the usual suspects, i.e. Far Right groups or Neo-Nazis. Rather the perpetrators are white, middle-class liberals, who are desperate to show that they are anything *but* racist. Lanre Bakare perfectly sums this up in his review:

> The kind of people who shop at Trader Joe's, donate to the ACLU and would have voted for Obama a third time if they could. Good people. Nice people. Your parents, probably. The thing Get Out does so well – and the thing that will rankle with some viewers – is to show how, however unintentionally, these same people can make life so hard and uncomfortable for black people. It exposes a liberal ignorance and hubris that has been allowed to fester. It's an attitude, an arrogance which in the film leads to a horrific final solution, but in reality leads to a complacency that is just as dangerous. (28 February 2017: *The Guardian*)

This as we will go onto see eerily parallels, yet beautifully captures, the same logics of the white, British, liberal university. That is, an institution guided by the same set of white liberal principles, performances, and practices. Since watching the film every time that I drive to my leafy suburban white campus, I have never been able to quite shake off the chill down my spine… and as this chapter will go onto demonstrate, the white liberal racism that continues to plague British universities is perhaps the most unsettling, the most isolating, and the most dangerous…

*   *   *

The university space is a difficult terrain for many racially marked academics to navigate. Universities are categorically coded as white spaces, as Sara Ahmed reminds us, the institution is orientated around whiteness, whereby non-white bodies are required to 'inhabit whiteness' if they are to be accepted (2007: 158). The institutionalization of whiteness produces a form of 'likeness' that leads to the discomfort, exposure, and vulnerability, of racialized bodies whose differences are both marked and (in)visibilized when they enter spaces governed by whiteness (ibid.). Whiteness refers not simply to phenotypical characteristics and origin, but rather represents complex structures of power, entitlement, and status (Patel 2017: 16). It describes a social positioning that is both structurally and racially privileged, benefitting those belonging to its category economically, socially, culturally, and politically (Sian 2017: 7). It defines itself as the norm and renders others 'abnormal,' invisible, or marginal (Garner 2010: 118–128). The university perhaps represents one of the key sites in which hegemonic forms of whiteness are reproduced and maintained. However, because the university also operates under the guise of a liberal model—i.e. 'progressive'—its racism and enactment of white supremacy is much more sophisticated in some ways.

To elaborate, the university is an institution whereby subtle forms of racism are more likely to occur—i.e. I would have voted for Obama— rather than the direct insults people of colour may encounter on the street, or on public transportation. In the white academy, insults are often replaced with a politics of exclusion, which works to situate the body of colour firmly on the outside; this is one of the defining characteristics of institutional racism. In the UK, institutional racism was 'officially' incorporated into mainstream policy discourse with the Macpherson Report (1999), which highlighted police failings following the racist murder of Stephen Lawrence (Hesse 2004: 131). One of the key recommendations of the report was that police should identify an incident to be racist if one of the parties or third party described the episode as racist/racially motivated. At the core of this subjective understanding was a conceptualization that saw racism, not as a specific system of oppression, but rather, as the more generalized product of a clash of members from different ethnic and racial groups. This paradoxically weakened the structural element of institutional racism (Sian et al. 2013: 33).

Rather than reading institutional racism through Macpherson's definition, I prefer to understand the category as one that is linked to practices of racial governance (Hesse 2004: 143). That is, institutional racism refers to structural practices that systematically affect the prospects of people of colour (Patel 2017: 126). It encompasses a set of hidden racist values, practices, and customs, that form the institutional norms of structures and organizations, and is closely associated with white privilege (ibid.). This subtle form of racism is defined by Barnor Hesse as, 'that which is concealed, hidden, disguised, unacknowledged, denied but which is consistent in its impact of strategic effect' (2004: 144). Manifestations of institutional racism can as such be found with the way in which experiences of racism are patterned both through structural conditioning and everyday interactions.

These everyday interactions can perhaps be read most clearly through 'racial microaggressions.' For Sue et al. racial microaggressions are defined as:

> …Brief and commonplace daily verbal, behavioral, or environmental indignities, whether intentional or unintentional, that communicate hostile, derogatory, or negative racial slights and insults toward people of color. Perpetrators of microaggressions are often unaware that they engage in such communications when they interact with racial/ethnic minorities. (Sue et al. 2007: 273)

Subtle practices of racism in the form of microaggressions are often more challenging because they operate against the common sense understanding of racism as easily identifiable. As such, the vague nature of racial microaggressions helps to disguise racism, making it less recognizable as they tend not to fall within the conventional remit of 'clear intentionality' which we see commonly associated with blatant acts of racism (Reid and Birchard 2010: 479; Essed 1991: 72–80; Sian 2017: 5). My interview data reveals the multilayered performances of microaggressions operating in universities, and the ways in which they are intensely bound up with practices of institutional racism.

My respondents had much to say about their day-to-day life in the academy and their experiences of everyday 'hidden' forms of racism. However, following on from Ahmed, it is important to note that the emotions expressed by my participants are not simply translated into a matter of 'psychological dispositions,' but rather, they will be understood as complex political discourses, that illuminate the intricate and textured relationships operating between the emotional, the social, and the cultural, at both the individual and collective level (2004: 119). What we see in the responses are really quite telling about both the way in which racism is enacted in the white university, and also how it is perceived, embodied, and lived by racially marked academics. There were key recurring themes across the interview data which all overlapped to fundamentally describe exclusionary practices of (liberal) racism.

Liberal Racism and Differential Treatment

In the British university, liberal racism is perhaps the most dominant form of racism practised by white members of staff. For Eduardo Bonilla-Silva, liberal racism, or what he characterizes as 'colourblind racism' takes the form 'racism lite' or 'smiling face discrimination' (2003: 3). That is, a new etiquette has developed whereby direct racial insults are, 'absent except ironically' (Sian et al. 2013: 6). This 'racism without racists' logic is the hallmark of liberal racism, which works to mask the realities of racism, while at the same time, reinforcing structures of white privilege (ibid.). As Zamudio and Rios suggest, 'relying on liberal principles as central to the colorblind race project works to deny the existence of the structural disadvantage of people of colour, while simultaneously obscuring the structural advantage or embedded racial privilege of whites' (2006: 487). What is essentially being described is the contemporary signification of the post-racial.

The post-racial put simply refers to '…the end of racism and its expulsion from the public domain' (Sian et al. 2013: 12). Over the years, universities have been central in reinforcing post-racial politics through agendas that deem anti-racism unnecessary and outdated. This can be seen through the undermining of race equality in all its senses; from an absence of systematic training and monitoring, to the scrapping of race-related subject courses—anti-racism is firmly off the agenda in higher education. Subsequently, the post-racial logic has steadily become hegemonic in organizing the shape and the very culture of universities. The idea that we are 'over race' is precisely how racism is sustained, that is, the dismissal or trivialization of racism operates to both facilitate and embolden it (Ahmed 2012: 182–183; Goldberg 2013: 15–18). In addition to this as David Theo Goldberg argues, articulations of the post-racial work to shift the collective responsibility of racism onto individuals, thus denying the structural nature of racism (2013: 17). The liberal, post-racial culture of denial, operating within British universities, has therefore meant that the daily realities of racism experienced by racially marked academics, are obscured and difficult to pin down, as white members of staff are unable to conceive of themselves as perpetrators of racism.

Bonilla-Silva's 'smiling face discrimination' perhaps best sums up the kinds of microaggressions that racially marked academics encounter within the university. My respondents were very aware of the prevalence of liberal racism in their institutions, as one respondent noted:

People in HE (Higher Education) like to pose as liberals, as if they're intelligent people, nice people – but they're not and that's the tragedy of it. Racism is much more insidious in HE. Remember what Malcolm X said: 'I have far more respect for a man who lets me know where he stands even if he is wrong, then the one who comes up like an angel but is nothing but a devil' that is imprinted on my mind. It's this idea that they don't want to look bad that gets to me the most. (Interview 9)

The notion that white colleagues are more nuanced in their exercise of racism—as they are keen to present themselves as 'nice,' 'respectable,' and 'tolerant' individuals—was also echoed by another respondent who said:

> People in academia are a bit smarter, they're more subtle, and they under-stand what they can't say. Everything is just a bit more institutionalized. But you get the sense that it's also the place where things are unchecked, it's a lot less frank... I think in general people try to be nice and they want to be nice but they have all these ingrained biases. (Interview 3)

The next respondent similarly expressed the following:

> There is a problem with how your colleagues perceive you. Many of them reproduce prejudicial attitudes refracted through their class position and privilege. So they can all read the Guardian, and say that they're against racism, but they can't see it in their own protocol and practices. My expe-rience is that colleagues are uncomfortable rather than downright hostile, unless they're semi-drunk and the mask begins to slip. And most of it is done by assumptions, double takes, and that English middle class dis-comfort around diversity. (Interview 5)

It was also argued by another participant that liberal racism (often masked as 'reasonableness'), allows white faculty members to assign heavier workload tasks to racially marked academics:

> Academics being the way they are politically- not as radical as they think- but generally more liberal in a small 'l' sense, believe that they hold a kind of reasonableness, and that comes into things like a workload dis-cussion, where they'll casually say, 'oh you can do that, you will be fine' so it's very much 'lets all get on with these things and lets all be agreeable'. (Interview 17)

The next respondent further describes how the particular performances or language of racism takes on a certain register in the university setting:

> You think that academia is the bastion of progression and so on, but if anything its just a particular materialisation of the day-to-day racism that I felt growing up, it's just the words, and the vernacular that are different in the university. (Interview 14)

My participants frequently felt that such enactments of liberal racism produced hidden forms of differential treatment, which in most cases could not be placed as direct discrimination due to their very subtleties:

> The problem with the day-to-day encounters of racism is that it's difficult to pinpoint them down. I've felt that I've not been included a number of times, or I am the last person to be consulted on something. And the more powerful or elite those discussions are, the more likely you are not to be included - so you hear about stuff later on. It's really that feeling of not being part of shaping the place you work. (Interview 20)

The same participant goes onto say:

> Sometimes it's just so damn subtle. It's in the gestures, it's in what's not said, and it's when you're one-on-one with people versus how they are when they're with other people - the treatment can be night and day with some. There are some people who will say hi to me when they're with a group of others in the faculty, but one-on-one in a hallway they don't even look up. (Interview 20)

This notion around the subtlety of racism in universities was strong across all my interviewees, who were very aware of being unable to 'prove' or 'evidence' that the particular act, gesture, or incident, was racist, for example one participant said:

> I've had problems with my line manager which I feel is motivated by the fact that I'm the only non-white staff member, and I've always had the feeling he doesn't like me very much, but then how do you prove or evidence that? This is the insidious side of the racism in universities - you

have to suffer it slowly, because you can't touch it, you can't hold it, you can't grasp it and you can't shake it; it's just there. (Interview 13)

What the respondents seem to be pointing at is a sense of being perceived and therefore positioned as second class citizens. This ascribed inferior status results in differential treatment such as not being included in discussions, being ignored, or simply not being liked (Sue et al. 2008: 336). The subjective nature of these experiences means that the participants encounter difficulties in trying to 'evidence' racism, thus the elusiveness of liberal racism means that responses and challenges to it are limited. This is a common feature of everyday life for people of colour, as Sue et al. describe, 'being overlooked in store lines, being passed by cabs, and having change put on the counter instead of in one's hand' (ibid.)—these are all subtle indicators of the ways in which racially marked individuals occupy a subordinate position in relation to dominant forms of whiteness.

There was also a strong sense of differential treatment being performed through regulatory and disciplinary practices, as one respondent noted:

> The racism I've encountered has been of a very different order. It's particular assumptions made about your intellectuality, your expertise, about how you teach and so on. It might not be something that's necessarily meant to denigrate you, but there's a degree of scrutiny that's reserved for certain types of people. (Interview 18)

The sense of being subjected to greater levels of inspection was also clear in the next response:

> Rather than racism articulate itself in a way where I'm being called bad things, it's almost like a subtle kind of attitude that seems to place me as an outsider. One colleague of mine has to be the dominating figure, almost like she knows best, even though she's only been in post one year longer than me. I constantly feel like she's challenging everything that I try to do, and I don't know whether that's because she thinks I'm incompetent because I'm a man of colour… it's almost a bit insulting. (Interview 4)

The designation of people of colour as subjects that require disciplining is a key component of western racial histories. The disciplining and regulation of racialized populations has been practised since the birth of the European colonial enterprise (i.e. slavery, forced sterilization, Black Codes, segregation) and has continued through to the present via mass incarceration, policing, and migration policies, to name but a few. It should come as no surprise then, that racially marked academics in the university experience daily attempts by white liberal colleagues to regulate and surveil their bodies, as Nirmal Purwar points out, 'the slightest glitch in their work performance turns the awe and fascination about their appointment to disappointment that warrants special surveillance and disciplinary measures' (2004: 54). This will be picked up in more detail when I explore the construction of racially marked academics as 'troublemakers,' however it is worth noting that in both these instances both academics felt like they were being scrutinized and judged around their competence, intellect, and ability. This again works to reinforce assumptions around racially marked academics as being somehow 'inferior' to their white counterparts.

Interestingly, in the above response, it is a white female academic that is seeking to undermine and 'guide' a racially marked male academic. This was a persistent theme throughout my interviews, and was experienced both at the departmental level in different contexts, as well as within teaching spaces. White (middle class, liberal) women have historically occupied a dominant position in relation men of colour. Transatlantic slavery established the dehumanization of black men through two key registers. On the one hand they were emasculated, depicted as 'infantile,' and on the other they were paradoxically read as hyper-masculine, violent, and 'savage,' as Vron Ware argues, such constructions, 'derive their meanings from the historical memory produced by centuries of slavery and colonization' (Ware 1996: 81). The incident that my participant described can be seen as a replaying of those broader racial histories, 'in which black men were denied respect...and reduced to caricatures - rendered childlike' (Yancy 2017: 2). The white woman's desire to therefore correct, instruct, challenge, and dominate the brown man is closely attached to earlier white supremacist discourses that impose inferiority upon men of colour.

My male participants stated that they felt that the most common perceptions of racially marked men in the university—held by white liberal female (often feminist) academics—included: 'hyper-patriarchal,' 'sexist,' 'oppressive,' 'threatening,' 'dangerous,' 'homophobic,' 'too religiously inclined,' 'overly familiar,' 'excessively confident,' 'jocular,' 'young,' and 'lacking in ability.' On the other hand, racially marked female academics also complained that white female academics tended to be dismissive, patronizing, and critical, often framing them as weak and subordinate. Such practices are perhaps more pronounced in the social sciences as they can be linked closely to the development of white feminist discourse. Conventional white feminism has persistently dismissed and misrepresented the complex experiences of both women and men of colour, due to its narrow focus on white, straight, able-bodied, middle-class women (Garner 2010: 36). Such an articulation of 'liberal' feminism has not only meant that white women have claimed the monopoly of victimhood (Madriz 1997), but moreover, it has actively legitimized racism through the exercise of imperial thought and practice (Mohanty 1988), which has operated to domesticate and discipline communities of colour, the most obvious example here is continued attempts to 'liberate' Muslim women from their 'oppressive' Muslim men.

The re-enactment of these highly problematic constructs in academic spaces by white women, appear to work as a means to preserve their own privilege, and re-establish colonial ideas of whiteness as the norm. Here I think Vron Ware offers an important analysis in relation to white feminist politics and the historical memory of empire. She rightly argues that:

> The danger that arises from overlooking the 'often silent and hidden operations' of racial domination throughout women's histories poses a threat to the survival of feminism as a political movement. For it is partly through the returning to the past that we are able to understand how those categories of difference between women and men, white and non-white, have emerged and how, why and where they continue to retain significance. (1996: 154)

In order for white feminists to show solidarity with racialized groups in the academy (and beyond), and with both men and women, it is paramount that they reflect seriously upon their own privilege and complicity in perpetuating toxic racist discourses at both conceptual and everyday levels. Ware suggests that feminist politics, 'must be able to intervene in debates about contemporary politics with a historically informed and anti-racist perspective' (ibid.). If gendered racism in universities is to be disrupted, white, liberal, female academics perhaps need to critically examine the role that they play in the exercise of symbolic forms of violence, power, and privilege.

What we have seen throughout this section is the way in which liberal racism has been performed through exclusionary processes and differential treatment. As my participants have described, this form of racism in the academy is commonplace, yet the idealization of the 'post-racial, liberal university' has allowed for it to be obscured, and consequently lacking in both importance and significance. Herein lies the problem.

The Troublemaker

Historically, people of colour have been persistently represented by western nations as posing a 'threat' to the preservation of white hegemony. As previously sketched out the black male has suffered centuries of vilification through racialized and criminalizing discourses, this continuation can be seen namely in the over-representation of racially marked males in the criminal justice system (Hall et al. 2013; Davis 2003). Attached therefore to the male body of colour, is a particular set of racializing characteristics signifying 'anger,' 'violence,' 'antagonism,' and 'irrationality.' These constructs however are not just confined to racially marked males; females too have also had to endure the label of 'angry woman of colour.' White notions of black anger have served as regulatory mechanisms throughout history to restrict and prevent the agency of people of colour. These racist ideas play out on racialized bodies particularly when they are active, that is when they challenge, organize, and mobilize (i.e. civil rights movement, black feminist movement, black lives matter). Their expression is therefore rarely (if ever) read in the mainstream as legitimate, in other words, they do not represent agents for social change that seek to resist systems of white supremacy, but rather, they are read by white society as those 'deliberately' disrupting social order, and 'purposefully' provoking response and reaction. It therefore becomes the 'duty' of white actors to manage, monitor, and discipline people of colour.

The manifestation of this performance in universities is astounding, yet hardly surprising from a cynical point of view. My respondents, both men and women, were very aware that they were likely to encounter white colleagues attempting to position them as troublesome and disruptive. They were also conscious of having to try and counteract and escape such labelling which operates to debilitate them within the system. Respondents spoke of feelings of being under-surveillance by their white peers and students, that is, they felt that they were monitored, critiqued, and scrutinized, to a much greater degree because they were racially marked. As one respondent recalled:

> The visibility I experience is surveillance and monitoring. So it's not even an honest curiosity or investment in who you are or your scholarship, it is more like monitoring what you are doing- assessing you for threats, that's what it feels like. Whether it's a threat to risk management because you're assumed to be shady, or a threat to them personally and professionally – so if you're out-doing them, in this sense you can be visible but not more successful then them. So the visibility is very much an assessment of threat. (Interview 20)

The participant clearly feels that her white colleagues are vetting her. This vetting process entails several layers. On the one hand, the vetting takes place at the senior management level, whereby her body undergoes evaluation and identification for the potential risks that her blackness may present to the institution. On the other hand, her white colleagues closely monitor her performance, whereby she carries the burden of being a threat if she over-exceeds their expectations. She clearly feels subjected to their pre-emptive powers, perceived as risky and dangerous. These pre-emptive measures and risk management processes enacted by the university are familiar to the practices found within the criminal justice system, which rely upon the same set of procedures when 'dealing with' racially marked groups. That is, the regulation and disciplining of people of colour—commonly defined as a 'risk group'—generates pre-emptive criminalization of communities regardless of actual criminality (e.g. stop and search) (Fitzgibbon 2007: 135). In the university this can be seen with longer probation periods or additional teaching observations (Purwar 2004: 54). What we can see within the university is therefore a mirroring of the criminal justice system in attempts to both criminalize and discipline racially marked academics.

Another respondent said the following in relation to the way in which racially marked male academics in particular, are perceived as 'problematic' by the white institution:

> I think racialized men are seen as most problematic, because they are presumed to carry a degree of aggression, swagger, loudness – things of this sort. So you are read as threatening, intimidating, hostile and loud. Our presence is overstated, merely by being there. (Interview 18)

As Ahmed reminds us, ideas of aggression, intimidation, or hostility, operate to inscribe a 'negative value' on racially marked bodies, and they often 'carry the weight' of violent racial histories (2012: 159). These signifiers also become key mechanisms for white actors to locate the individual of colour as having 'racial baggage' (ibid.). Similar feelings were articulated by other respondents when describing how they felt that they were positioned in academic spaces:

> I think I'm seen at the very least as difficult, colleagues probably prefer it if I'm not in a meeting. If we say something that is counter-hegemonic, then we look as though we are problematic or antagonistic. If I challenged everything I wanted to, I don't think I'd have my job anymore. I've challenged an awful lot; it's exhausting. (Interview 12)

Another participant who was aware that he 'had to be careful' about the way in which he reacted in certain situations echoed this sentiment:

Something that I always ponder is how much to rock the boat in higher education. I'm seen to be 'outspoken' and often find myself having to manage my reaction in particular incidents. How you respond can place you as the 'aggressor' and the person who is at fault. So I'm always weary of that and being labelled the angry brown person. (Interview 13)

Ahmed suggests that particular forms of difference are read as assertive (i.e. rocking the boat), while other forms of difference (i.e. saying something counter-hegemonic), are viewed as deliberate acts of provocation (2012: 208). Beneath the various shades of expression, the underlying narrative that appears to be forming is around the way in which racially marked academics are (un)able to perform their agency, which carries consequences depending on the extent to which such agency is expressed.

The 'angry person of colour' label came up frequently across my interviews:

We always have to think about what we say, but I suspect white colleagues don't have to think, or feel conscious, in the same way as us. There are a lot of times when I'm thinking do the staff and students perceive me as a black radical? This is not a good position to be in within the university, certainly not in my institution. And that's quite uncomfortable because people might not listen to me, and focus instead on, 'that's just an angry black man,' I'm conscious all the time of this. I have to try and keep my emotions together so I'm not perceived as an angry black man. (Interview 10)

This was echoed by another respondent who felt that his colleagues perceived him to have 'a chip on his shoulder,' as a result he secluded himself from other members of staff, and felt the need to suppress his thoughts and ideas:

I have tried to make myself invisible and I have often felt like I have had to self-censor. I felt there was a sense that I had a chip on my shoulder so I often self-isolated as a result. (Interview 14)

Ahmed points to the way in which the 'familiar figure' of the 'angry person of colour' is a presence that always seems to be lurking in the background, and when a person of colour enters a particular space (i.e. a classroom or a meeting etc.), the figure has already appeared (ibid.: 209). She argues that when people of colour do turn up, and if there is friction, *they* (the body of colour) become the source of hostility often read as 'the one who is tense' (ibid.). As has been demonstrated, racially marked academics are seen to be 'responsible' for any conflict or tension arising within these settings, rather than wider structures and everyday performances of white supremacy. The blame is thus seen to lay with the racially marked body as opposed to institutional practices of racism, and those who are seen to be even mildly critical are likely to encounter closer inspection, as one respondent argues:

> I think being outspoken or willing to challenge certain issues related to race makes me more subjected to scrutiny and surveillance by colleagues. (Interview 13)

Another participant felt that his area of research and teaching aroused particular perceptions within his colleagues that positioned him as difficult or too critical, leading to further monitoring:

> I'm constantly under threat, and under psychological strain and pressure when doing my job because of the area I work within in the social sciences. As a result I'm often seen as being critical or challenging and that makes me more vulnerable to being watched more closely by colleagues. (Interview 4)

The threat of being under surveillance by white colleagues in the university was seen to also occur in the absence of active critiquing or challenging, that is, just the very presence of blackness or difference was felt to warrant further inspection:

> I have felt what I was doing in my social life was watched far more closely than it would be for my white colleagues. (Interview 12)

As mentioned in the previous section, surveillance can be seen as a key form of colonial governance to manage racialized bodies and maintain authority and dominance (Coleman and McCahill 2011). The university has therefore not been immune from adopting these colonial inspired surveillance practices to keep close watch over racially marked academics. As Purwar argues, the smallest of mistakes in their performance can be used as evidence to demonstrate that the individual is not fit for the job (2004: 54). This can subsequently lead to the legitimization of greater surveillance, 'with observations becoming closer and closer' (ibid.). Purwar goes onto suggest that such close monitoring leaves very little (if at all any) room for error, thus the institution is likely to find the particular fault(s) in the individual confirming its racially based assumptions (ibid.). Burdens of this kind—as the respondents alluded to above—can leave racially marked academics withdrawing into themselves, or feeling under immense pressure to perform, which in itself may cause mistakes by inducing unnecessary strain.

Our bodies in the university can be seen to represent key sites upon which white judgement, white regulation, and white resentment, are each played out, time and time again, lest we resist… Our anger—although always misunderstood, over-represented, and over-exaggerated, by our white colleagues—can also become an important tool for strength and creativity, and I do think it's worth acknowledging that in racist environments our anger *is* legitimate. Here I am reminded in particular of the powerful words of George Yancy when he writes, '…anger grounds me; it keeps me focused. Anger can provide clarity, especially within a context where my blackness is taken as sufficient evidence that I am guilty of something, that I am disposable' (2017: 3). As important as it is to disrupt the reductive and pathologizing narrative of 'angry person of colour,' perhaps it is just as important that when we are angry (which we have every right to be), we do not punish ourselves, or dismiss those feelings out of fear, but rather we embrace those emotions and experiences, to develop a rich pool of resources, that help to both uplift us and guide us through harmful, white academic spaces.

Everyday Otherness: 'We All Look the Same'

Racially marked academics are continually subjected to processes of othering at both the structural and interpersonal level. Through crude practices of racialization, we encounter judgment, exoticization, and demonization, through various phenotypical, cultural, and religious symbols, attached to our bodies and *being*. Edward Said's (1978) critique of Orientalism is of clear relevance here for understanding the dynamics through which power/knowledge is exercised as an attempt to domesticate racially marked academics in the university setting. The British university as a fundamentally colonial institution means that it can only be predicated upon Orientalist logics and imaginings. As Said demonstrates, Western academia has been central in both the maintenance and the perpetuation of the (violent) distinction between the Orient and the Occident, that is, 'Orientalism lives on academically through its doctrines and theses about the Orient and the Oriental' (Said 1978: 2). Orientalism is thus woven into the very structures of the university, and operates to embed and reproduce Western dominance, through the subordination of the subaltern, both symbolically and systemically.

The distinction between, self and other ('we'/'they') can not only be found explicitly in the Eurocentric curriculum,[2] but also in the actual make-up of the institution itself, whereby the presence of the other is overwhelmingly absent and silenced. As David Tyrer suggests, 'there is a continued investment in the idea that our Others possess an excess of alterity which threatens the wider polity and needs to be tamed and domesticated through integration' (2013: 102). Tyrer goes onto argue that underlying this narrative is the notion that difference is not challenging merely because it is different, but rather because it represents, or signifies a threat (ibid.). We saw in the previous section some of the ways in which the 'threat' of the other is managed through practices of surveillance and hyper-scrutiny, however, we will go on to see that this is also enacted via everyday exclusionary interactions that seek to mark out difference, while simultaneously diluting its presence. In other words, the university, and its white staff cohort, appear to collectively take charge in the 'handling' of difference and diversity, to ensure that it is 'manageable' (i.e. a splash of colour), rather than 'excessive.' The continuous pointing out of otherness by white colleagues (often understood as unusual, exotic, unfitting and inappropriate), represents the exceptionality of difference in the academy. This works as a reminder that racially marked academics are marginal, they do not belong, and for the most part they are compelled to comply with, and assimilate into, the white university culture to ensure that they don't pose a threat.

Feelings of otherness, marginality (as a result of otherness), and white discomfort around difference, were common for my respondents. There was a gendered particularity here, in that the majority of those who articulated specific instances of otherness tended to be overwhelmingly racially marked female academics. Racially marked male academics focused more on their experiences of hyper-visibility, which will be examined further in the next section. The majority of my respondents spoke of experiences around: Being mistaken for the only other racially marked academic, difficulties with white colleagues (mis)pronouncing their name, issues around language and attire, exoticization, and cultural appropriation. In terms of being mistaken for the only other person of colour, one respondent recalls:

> There's always the thing of being confused with the only other person of colour, even when you're completely different, it's really strange, when we don't look similar or our names are not even similar. It's so strange that some people make that particular link because of our ethnicity. And this has happened to me at a conference, when somebody called me the name of the other person of colour also organizing the conference, and I was like, 'oh that's not my name' and he said 'oh, oh it's because of the hair', and he'd obviously realised what he'd done but then I felt like I had to help him manage his embarrassment in that situation. I was embarrassed, he was embarrassed, but in addition to coping with my embarrassment I felt I had to help him so he didn't look as silly as he did. (Interview 16)

I remember we both burst out laughing at this part in the interview, because our experiences had been so similar. The laughter was the outcome of the shared sense of disbelief (and exhaustion) that our white colleagues were actually that ignorant, unaware, and oblivious, to their practices of power and privilege. In my own experiences, being mistaken for the only other female academic of colour has been a common occurrence. I have honestly lost count of the number of times that I have been in meetings and senior colleagues have asked me a question while addressing me with the name of the only other female academic of colour (despite me working at that institution for a number of years! And despite me looking nothing like that person). Of course, they go red in the face and then try to pass it off as a joke and call a white colleague a different name (read—see I do it to them too!) in a desperate attempt to diffuse the situation and recover from their sense of embarrassment. Or they will blame it on a long day and swiftly move on. As the respondent mapped out, so often is the case that we are left to not only deal with our embarrassment, but we are then required to reassure and support the perpetrator to save them from their feelings of humiliation. Nowadays when I am not addressed with the correct name, I often watch with amusement at their discomfort as they try and escape the fact that they have made the rookie mistake of assuming that 'we all look the same'—perhaps one of the most explicit displays of racism, just behind 'my best friend is black.'

These practices of mistaking have also occurred when senior white colleagues have addressed me in emails by the name of the only other academic of colour, furthermore I have had letters in my pigeonhole not addressed to me but—you guessed it—to the only other person of colour in the department. The frequency of this particular faux pas by both academic and administrative staff is indicative of the racism lurking beneath the 'liberal' university, in which white colleagues like to claim that they are tolerant, and certainly not racist, however when confronted with an immediate situation they can only revert back to their ingrained biases symptomatic of a wider institutional racism. Not only does this demonstrate their incapacity to invest in racially marked academics (i.e. addressing them with the correct name!), but it also illustrates their discomfort around difference.

The irony of course is that my parents gave me a highly anglicized name in the naive hope that by assimilating my difference, racism would magically disappear. There is a sense of sadness (directed at racism, not my parents) that my ethnicity had to be obscured through my name in order to 'fit in.' I entirely respect and understand their decision which is symptomatic of their own realities of discrimination, thus for my parents this served as a coping strategy and a means to try and protect their children from racism in the absence of tools. Regardless, my experiences quite clearly shows that having a racially marked name or not, does most certainly not make a difference; it does not make one immune from the workings of racism within racist institutions like the university.

The othering through mistaking, or having 'difficult' names causing issues around mispronunciation, came up time and time again in my interviews, as one respondent said:

> You feel like you are foreign. Most people in the department can't pronounce or spell my name right. Often white males would be particularly bad at asking how to pronounce my name, or trying. And the funny thing is they feel so comfortable mispronouncing my name; they just don't seem to feel any hesitance, or embarrassment about pronouncing my name wrong, because it's not important enough. This makes you feel even more distant from members of staff. It's like they can't even say your name, so it puts another layer of distance between you and them. (Interview 1)

Here we see the way in which particularly white male academics do not even feel the need to learn the respondents name, rather she feels that they are comfortable actually saying it incorrectly because her presence is deemed insignificant. This exclusionary form of othering not only works to locate her as different, but also sends the message that her very *being* is irrelevant and inconsequential to the department. As I previously mentioned, this is illustrative of the lack of investment in racially marked academics. These daily encounters place us as marginal; they silence us and consistently devalue us. Another respondent spoke of a similar experience:

> I am mixed, a lot of people think that I'm white, but when people do read me as other I'm exotic, or when people hear my accent and see my name, they know instantly that I'm not from here, but they can't place me —so I'm always in between… I always get mistaken for another staff

member of colour, because they're so few of us, even though these people look nothing like me. It's just so odd; it just works as a reminder.
(Interview 2)

The exoticization of the respondents' subjectivity is characteristic of
Orientalism. This is prevalent especially among women of colour, whose
racialized construction locates them as a 'particular oriental other' via
practices of racial, imperial, and patriarchal domination (Patel 2017:
94). Exoticization has thus become a central defining feature of women
marked as other (ibid.). The 'reminder' that the participant alludes to
in her response, suggests that she does not belong; she is not considered
'one of them.' Her ability to initially 'pass' due to her ethnic unmarking,
fails to travel very far, because she is immediately marked by her accent
and her name, this is again indicative of the way in which racism, and
racist assumptions, can never be offset. In other words, an English name
cannot counteract brown skin; similarly 'light' skin cannot counteract
'different' (non-Western) accents or 'difficult' (non-Western) names. No
matter the mix of ethnic marking and unmarking,[3] the fact remains
that whiteness can only read others through a racialized grammar, that
someway or another, will eventually group us as all together as essentially being 'the same.' The issue of non-English accents was picked up
by another respondent who said:

There is a huge issue around accents in British universities; both white
staff and students are very uncomfortable hearing an accent that is not
English. Students and staff do take an issue with your accent, and because
you are of colour it is assumed that you cannot communicate properly.
Why should I be impeached because of my accent? This comes up in a
subtle manner, time and time again. (Interview 19)

Many of my participants echoed this sentiment, and expressed a particular sense of Englishness pervading the academy, that manifests itself
as superior (Sian 2017: 9). Englishness refers to a set of exclusionary
practices and values intertwined with articulations of whiteness and
constructions of others as inferior in aptitude and temperament (ibid.).
It assumes the exceptionality of England in world history and culture,

exemplifying a unique set of manners, traditions, and customs, associated with England as a liberal economy and polity (ibid.; Hall 2014: 57–58). As a result, white English members of staff presume that lessons on pronunciation, history, and culture, are required for those whose first language is not English:

> Often when we eat lunch together, there is one senior member of staff who —towards me and a Chinese member of staff particularly— likes explaining a lot, so we'll be in a group, he'll be talking, and then he'll often pause and look at me, and say 'Do you understand?' or 'Do you know what I mean?' And it becomes really embarrassing. In a group of people it is super patronizing. It's not only about words, it's also about events, or famous or historical English people. He just assumes that I won't know. (Interview 1)

The same respondent feels that her difference serves as a transitory topic for discussion and critique by her white colleagues (Sian 2017: 9). The superficial engagement with her difference reaffirms Orientalist narratives whereby her home country is seen as either a tourist attraction or a space of backwardness (ibid.), as she goes onto describe:

> If you are different, your difference goes only in a way to satisfy people's interests, so that might be a current political debate, or a place they once visited. But when your difference means that they have to do some work, like learn your name, that means they have to do labour and they are not prepared to do that, which tells me that they're not prepared to embrace that difference. So it's about taking your difference and making it the interesting topic to be discussed at lunch, where you talk about how 'backwards' Polish people are, and 'oh these laws are terrible' and so on. (Interview 1)

Again we can see here white colleagues clearly partaking within processes of exoticization, whereby white, Western scholars are 'fascinated' by her 'different' culture; they are 'experts' and are keen to demonstrate their knowledge and interest in other cultures and countries (Patel 2017: 94). The problem with such fetishization lies in the fact that the interest is selective and shallow, which reproduces racism through the perpetuation of the Western gaze (ibid.). These Orientalist fantasies can also be seen manifested when concerning the way in which racially marked female academics, in particular, dress. For example one respondent said:

> I've often had remarks about my appearance, so my clothes or my style, which in any professional setting is a bit weird, especially by those you don't really know. (Interview 16)

The obsession with the way in which women of colour dress continues to haunt our subjectivity. In my own experiences, there has been a similar fascination around jewellery, make-up, and general comments about my being 'stylish'—and while white colleagues may think that they are being 'complimentary' or 'flattering,' for the most part it is actually highly inappropriate. These 'innocent' comments make us subjects of the western (predominantly male) gaze, which renders us 'other,' 'sexualized,' and 'desirable' (Patel 2017: 94). Such Orientalism manifests itself in a number of ways, including cultural appropriation:

> There's one particular white staff member who does a lot of cultural appropriation, which I find really uncomfortable. So she will wear ethnic dress or ethnic jewellery and so on. She always asks me where I got my earrings or my necklace from, and almost demands she has to have them. She's literally obsessed with particular non-Western cultures, it's just very weird. (Interview 6)

Once again we see clear themes of exoticization, fetishization, and fascination, being enacted by the white colleague in the above encounter. The adopting of particular aspects of non-Western cultures by members of the dominant culture is an exercise in coloniality, as Clara Gallini argues, cultural appropriation can be seen as both an act of acquisition/robbery that represents dominance, or it can give the (false) pretence of 'unchallenged forms of integration' (1996: 215). Cultural appropriation is also highly classed, as it is usually (white) bourgeois types that seek to add to their 'exotic' collection of artefacts, oblivious to their role in the perpetuation of imperial hierarchies (ibid.). However when the difference goes too far (i.e. 'excessive,' or 'threatening'), it can be quickly deemed less 'exotic' and more 'problematic,' as one participant found to be true in her experiences:

> I sometimes wear Asian dress and that marks me out as different. This brings out different reactions, and I've seen with staff that people will never accept me for who I am because I am seen as different. Because of my dress, white colleagues have ignored me, they have been rude to me, and they have questioned me, called me names and sniggered behind my back. I felt humiliated, while my other white colleagues have just laughed it off and trivialized it. It's been absolutely horrible, just because of what I chose to wear I am treated so differently. Constantly, there are sly comments my way. I never expected educated people to behave in such a way, it's disgraceful. (Interview 11)

In recent times the 'war on terror' has facilitated an increasingly hostile, Islamophobic climate. It has also brought a new set of racializing categories into being, whereby anything deemed 'overtly Asian' becomes equivalent to notions of Muslimness—which in itself has become synonymous with a range of essentializing signifiers including, 'submissive,' 'passive,' 'oppressive,' 'threatening,' 'backwards,' etc. Consequently 'excessive' displays of Asianness (typically read as Muslimness)—that go beyond earrings and bangles—are viewed with fear and hostility (Patel 2017: 95). Furthermore, as demonstrated in the above response, the performance of Islamophobia is not just confined to far-right extremist groups, but rather it also extends to supposedly 'educated' 'liberal' academics. The 'exotic gaze' in this context has thus been replaced by a 'hate gaze,' which seeks to dominate and domesticate through regulation, scrutiny, and intimidation (ibid.). The next section will draw out a number of themes which have been mapped out here, to highlight further the ways in which racially marked academics are simultaneously 'hyper-visiblized' and 'invisiblized' (Lander and Santoro 2017), in the white university.

The Only Person of Colour: Invisibility/Hyper-Visibility, 'Outsiders,' and (Non)Belonging

For racially marked academics invisibility paradoxically interplays with hyper-visibility, this is particularly heightened in the university setting whereby due to our absence within the institution, 'our very presence is a disruption' (hooks 1989: 19). The complex dynamic of invisibility and hyper-visibility operates to locate racially marked academics as 'outsiders,' whereby our difference is intensified because of our physicality within the space ("Look, a Negro!"),[4] yet simultaneously we are dismissed particularly within formal spaces because of our difference (i.e. in meetings). In other words, we are at the same time, both exceptionalized and marginalized. To understand hyper-visibility I want to elaborate further upon, and make clear the obvious relevance of Frantz Fanon's (1986) *Black Skin White Masks*, which enables us to critically think through the processes, practices, and impact of being a racially marked body in a white (violent) space (university). As Fanon argues, 'the black man will have no occasion to experience his being through others' (1986: 82), that is, the marked black subject is not afforded the opportunity to be anything other than black. As Fanon goes onto explain, '…not only must the black man be black; he must be black in relation to the white man' (ibid.: 83). In racist systems and societies, people of colour therefore can only be read and located *as* people of colour, whose existence or *being* is represented by and through whiteness, which does not permit or allow them to be more.

When Fanon describes an encounter in which a white child exclaims, 'Look, a Negro!' (ibid.: 82), we are presented with the explicit exercise of power and dominance (i.e. whiteness), that can only see and understand our (people of colour) *being* through racial and ethnic characteristics (as defined by whiteness). As Fanon expresses, 'I wanted to be a man, nothing but a man' (ibid.: 85). Whiteness thus violently objectifies our bodies, rendering us black before we are woman or man, black before we are short or tall, black before we are strong or weak, black before we are intelligent… black before we are anything else. As such we are expected to behave or perform *like* a person of colour, to ensure that whiteness is reinforced and validated (ibid.: 86). Ahmed alerts us to the fact that consequently, 'you have to be careful what you say, how you appear, to maximize the distance between you and their idea of you' (2012: 160). As sketched out previously particularly for men of colour, typical white expectations/assumptions include that they will behave in a 'threatening,' 'intimidating,' 'hostile,' and 'loud' manner.

Fanon speaks of the inescapable fact of his blackness, 'The evidence was there, unalterable. My blackness was there, dark and unarguable. And it tormented me, pursued me, disturbed me, angered me' (Fanon 1986: 88). The hyper-visibility that whiteness imposes upon people of colour operates to oppress us, and as we will see the interviewees strongly echo this sense of discomfort and suffering. Fanon in that moment understandably desires anonymity and invisibility, 'Look, I will accept the lot, as long as no one notices me!' (ibid.). It is worth emphasizing that the gendered nature of racism means that hyper-visibility in racially marked men is often far more pronounced (subject to context), that is, the encounters with racism that men of colour experience are often over-determined by their masculinity and the racial epithets attached to it (i.e. aggressiveness, antagonistic, angry, threatening, in other words hyper-masculinity). Hyper-visibility is not however just experienced by racially marked male academics, from the data it was clear that some racially marked female academics also felt that they were hyper-visible in the university. Furthermore, while hyper-visibility can indeed produce legitimate feelings of not wanting to be noticed, as we will go onto see the long-term effects of institutional invisibility can just be as debilitating.

The invisibility experienced by people of colour can be described as, 'an inner struggle with the feeling that one's talents, abilities, personality, and worth are not valued or even recognized because of prejudice and racism' (Franklin 1999: 761). Here the invisibility produced by whiteness is performed through the dismissing, devaluing, lessening and rejection of the racialized body. Fundamentally, it is a way of undermining their very existence through the failure to acknowledge their *being*.

Invisibility will often occur in a sustained and on-going fashion, to essentially exclude a person of colour within the given environment. Anderson J. Franklin describes this process as the 'invisibility syndrome' to which 7 key characteristics are attached. These include: (1) The subject experiences a lack of recognition or appropriate acknowledgment; (2) The subject feels no sense of satisfaction or gratification from the encounter (it is painful and injurious); (3) The subject self-doubts and questions their legitimacy (4) The subject feels invalidated and questions their self worth, or seeks some form of corroboration of experiences from another person; (5) The subject feels disrespected; (6) The subject's sense of dignity is compromised and challenged; and (7) The subject's identity is shaken, or uprooted (1999: 764). Because both hyper-visibility and invisibility are not mutually exclusive, but rather coexist to produce a set of incapacitating effects on racialized bodies, I would argue that the simultaneous process of hyper-visibility and invisibility—enforced by white structures and individuals—locates racially marked academics in what Fanon describes as the 'zone of nonbeing' (1986: 2). In other words, racially marked academics are systemically and symbolically dehumanized.

My interviewees expressed how such processes manifested as a means to single them out and silence or dismiss their contributions and very presence:

> I think physically I feel totally out of place, because I'm brown, I've got a beard and I'm a Muslim, I feel very visible. In HE I'm swimming in a sea of whiteness, and I stand out. However, I'm invisible at the same time, because people like me are nowhere to be seen, which means that my voice, my politics, and my ideas are dismissed, they don't care about them and they don't cater for them. (Interview 9)

Another respondent commented on being outright ignored by his colleagues:

> Often there are colleagues who I've met and then when I see them again they just don't acknowledge me. (Interview 13)

The next participant pointed to the ways in which racially marked academics are only apparent as a 'problem,' otherwise they remain silenced, particularly in positions of power:

As a male academic of colour, I am always having to deal with being visible or invisible. I notice this because I can see that we are under-represented where it matters. There is a culture of not recognizing our talents and contributions; so there is an attempt therefore to silence academics of colour. We are visible only when there is a problem, then for the most part our ideas and opinions are glossed over. (Interview 19)

Similarly:

I feel hyper-visible in my department because I am the only man of colour and that draws attention. But then I'm completely invisible when it comes to having a nice role in the department, or when it comes to receiving acknowledgement for my research. (Interview 13)

We can see clearly how the responses tie into experiences of being undervalued and ignored by colleagues and the institution. The next respondent speaks of the ways in which he is represented through discourses of whiteness whereby particular expectations are placed upon him as a racially marked academic:

I feel I'm hypervisible and two things really grate me. One is if you do racism, this is a personal experience matter, this is some kind of cultural literacy that has been bequeathed to us just merely by living, and the idea that this is actually an intellectual or scholarly pursuit, and all the hard learning and industry involved in that is put aside- something that is just natural. The other one, that I do resent, is that there is a certain kind of accommodation within academia where people who are racialized are assumed to do race, which in part is correct, but you are then designated only to that terrain. And the confidence that which you may speak on other things to which you are not racially designated is not taken into account, and that is frustrating actually. (Interview 18)

Here we are able to see how the respondent resents being continually read through a reductive lens, that is, a racially marked academic who only 'does race,' (i.e. hypervisibilized). These assumptions work to displace and dismiss (i.e. invisibilize), his extensive skills and competencies in different areas. In other words, he is constructed through a narrow framework imposed by whiteness, whereby he is the 'expert' on race (and not much more) because of his racialized subjectivity. This strongly echoes the research findings of Vini Lander and Ninetta Santoro, who in their study on the experiences of BME academics, found that participants, 'were simultaneously invisible and hypervisible with regard to their professional knowledge and standing' (2017: 1011), this worked to impact upon their self-confidence and sense of (in)ability.

The feeling of isolation was clear, whereby my participants expressed that because they were so few in number, they did not belong. This was a common complaint, particularly in the context of meetings whereby they were often the only person of colour present. This was reflected across a wide range of responses including:

> I was in a departmental meeting the other day - I think that there were about 30 other people in that meeting - and the only people of colour were me and a black guy. And it's not a nice feeling. (Interview 9)

> Being non-white, visibly non-white, I'm very conscious of my racialized status when I walk on campus - absolutely no doubt about that, it's uncomfortable. (Interview 10)

> There was a point in my department that the other person of colour turned around to me and said, 'you do realise there's only two of us right?' (Interview 17)

> There are a few people of colour in my department, but I still feel like I will often be the only one there because even if there's two or three of us, if one or two doesn't turn up to a meeting, I'm back to being totally on my own. (Interview 12)

> I always feel like an outsider in the academy…like I am the only one… my experience of the academy is that I'm a black man in a white world. All it takes is for you to go to a meeting and you immediately realise that the one thing that is missing here is colour - there is no colour…it's a colourless environment. (Interview 4)

There appears to be a strong resemblance across the interviews that points to the widespread nature of institutional racism. These acts unravel the ways in which subtle and structural processes of racism work to reinforce whiteness at the expense of racialized bodies; who both visible and invisible remain positioned as 'outsiders.' This 'outsider' status was also a prominent theme in research conducted by Kalwant Bhopal examining the experiences of BME academics (2016: 73). She found that power relations in the white academy operated to consistently exclude racially marked academics (2016: 73). The structures of the institution thus replay and reproduce the haunting 'Look, a Negro!' experience, which follows racially marked academics around in every crack and crevice, that is, there is no escape from suffocating, oppressive forms of whiteness that inhabit the university. The lack of other minorities within the institution makes those few present highly exposed, this in turn works to produce feelings of alienation, discomfort, and vulnerability. The university is not somewhere that one would typically expect to encounter black bodies, as a consequence, being a racially marked academic in predominantly white university spaces carries, 'emotional and psychological costs to the bearer of that difference' (Mirza 2006: 106). It is therefore perhaps not all too surprising that the sense exclusion, and feelings of non-belonging, remained a prevalent concern for my participants:

> I absolutely feel like I don't belong. In my department I'm the only non-white academic staff member and that's not easy. So I'm always conscious that I'm the only brown guy in the department and that's always a struggle and you do feel like an outsider. (Interview 13)

Similarly, another respondent said:

> Everywhere that I've worked I've been the only person of colour...I feel very visible, and very uncomfortable a lot of the time. I don't always instantly relate to what other people are talking about in terms of tastes and interests and views on the world. It has been quite isolating at times. (Interview 16)

As Lander and Santoro suggest in order for universities to facilitate change, academic and professional staff, as well as policymakers, must reflect upon and recognize how the positioning of BME academics as hyper-visible and invisible impacts upon their work, self-esteem, progression and status (2017: 1019). The next participant makes us aware of the double exclusion that she faces as a racially marked female academic. That is, the intertwining of her racial and gendered difference operates to further dismiss and silence her, and produces feelings of being undervalued and ignored:

> I feel out of place in my department for a number of reasons. One is because I am non-white. I believe that all the big name people in our department are white men. I feel out of place all the time as a result of that and where my expertise lies. Second I'm a woman, so I feel like my voice is not heard. I feel like I don't matter. There's a sense I'm ignored. (Interview 6)

Another respondent perhaps most poignantly reflected the sense of marginality that she felt as a racially marked academic:

> In the air you know and feel that your embodied presence does not belong- so there's nobody that looks like you up on the wall, there's nothing. This not only says you and your kind were never there, but also that there's no hope for you to ever be up on a wall. Even though some of us are in this space, it's like we've left nothing there to signal to the next black or brown girl that we were here. There's no remnant of us, because of the way that they protect these spaces, so it feels like maybe people of colour pass before me in these spaces, but there's no evidence of them ever being there. (Interview 20)

This response takes us back to Fanon's zone of nonbeing. Our presence, our contribution, and our significance as racially marked academics, ruthlessly disregarded, unrewarded…gradually eliminated. Collectively my interviewees show that even for the very few of us who do occupy the university space, we are never really truly 'there,' we do not belong. We may well be seen, but we are most definitely not heard which is symptomatic of the interplay between our visibility and invisibility.

The powerful work of bell hooks on notions of marginality and location is particularly resonant with the experiences outlined above. She helps us however to recognize that rather than seeing marginality, as solely representing a space of 'deprivation,' it can also become, 'the site of radical possibility, a space of resistance' (1989: 20). It is, as she describes, 'a central location for the production of a counter hegemonic discourse that is not just found in words but in the habits of being and the way one lives' (ibid.). Similarly, Patricia Hill-Collins has long examined and critiqued the marginality of Black women in academia, and social science disciplines. Collins argues that it remains vital that as racially marked female academics, we draw upon our experiences of being 'outsiders' to develop a distinct and rich analyses of race, gender and class, and in doing so, we become what she describes as 'outsiders within' (1986: S14–S15). Both hooks and Collins are inviting us to understand, and use our marginality, as a form of resistance to generate critical insight as a way to pierce and disrupt racist structures. Resistance in this way is thus crucial if we are to rebuild our sense of worth in a violent climate that persistently excludes, isolates, and dehumanizes us.

Self-doubt and 'Over-Sensitivity'

As we have seen, microaggressions provoke distress because they intentionally or unintentionally dismiss a person of colour, leading to isolation, perplexity, and a lack of belief in oneself (Franklin et al. 2006: 13). Microaggressions therefore represent a key practice of institutional racism, and as already demonstrated, they often operate implicitly, without the 'intent' to harm and without the recognition of privilege and power (Okazaki 2009: 104; Sian 2017: 6). As a result, such encounters of racism within the university setting can prompt racially marked academics to question and doubt that what they are experiencing is 'in fact' racism, as one respondent noted:

> I self doubt all the time when it comes to my experiences of racism. It makes me pause. I have to think firstly did it happen how I perceived it, and secondly how will others respond if I respond in a particular way? So you're already immediately self-conscious in terms of how others

perceive you, we know ethnic minorities are always accused of blowing things out of proportion. This affects people's self-esteem and confidence. (Interview 13)

The perpetual cycle of self-doubting and questioning was a process that the majority of my respondents had to deal with, as Purwar argues, because black bodies are not 'natural' in academia, they have to 'endure a burden of doubt' from those around them (2004: 53–54; Sian 2017: 7). This requires a great deal of emotional labour, and personal investment, whereby the incident encountered has to be interpreted and reinterpreted by the subjected (Ahmed 2012: 160). The next respondent expresses the cost of that labour, where she feels like she has to continuously assess herself, the situation, and the environment:

> I feel like I constantly evaluate myself, because I don't live my life with a race part on me that's self imposed, it's something that manifests through the interactions with other people, and it's because other people find it important. So I don't wake up being a black woman! But how other people interpret you is often with great difficulty, and you have to go through all these levels of analysis to decide if they have been a particular way towards you because of how they perceive you. And that's the harm of it too, because you have to second-guess everything, so who you are, the environment, and how you are interpreted - and how you yourself interpret interactions. (Interview 20)

Here we are alerted to the way in which the participant is forced into continuous self-evaluation as a result of the broader structures of racism that assign race to her body. When she says, 'I don't wake up being a black woman' we are reminded here again of Fanon, and the ways in which hegemonic forms of whiteness impose blackness upon her *being*. As a consequence, she is then required to carry that burden, and understand, or work out, how she is perceived by *them*. The different levels that such understandings entail are suggestive of the demanding nature, and investment required, to carry out this form of labour. Importantly the participant speaks of the harm or violence of self-doubt, because at the core of self-doubt is the questioning of oneself, ones legitimacy.

This was picked up by another respondent who spoke of the paralysing effects of infantilization as a result of the interplay between race, gender, and age, attached to her subjectivity. This operated to such an extent that it impacted upon her confidence and self-esteem, leading her to feel that she had to continually justify her legitimacy to her colleagues, while at the same time questioning her own competence:

> I feel like I'm not always taken very seriously. I feel like I am infantilized, and this entwines with my race, age and gender, so I don't even know how to unpack that. I know I don't look my age, but I actually just get annoyed because it takes away from all the things that I've achieved. It's no longer a compliment, it's almost like every time you meet someone, you have to justify why you're in the job you are, or how much you have done. It's almost a sense of disbelief, and you can see the little cogs working where people think, 'well how has she done all of that?' And so I have to always give a potted CV to almost justify what I have done. But others are just accepted for who they are without having to do all this justification. In terms of my self-confidence it is damaging. It's so exhausting. It's a lot of energy expended on this issue, but it's also quite paralysing because although I know it is most definitely discrimination, at the same time I can't help but think I'm not good enough for this. I think I'm seen as much more junior than I am, because I am an ethnic minority woman, but it's difficult to prove that. (Interview 16)

Here again, we are confronted with the labour involved in having to legitimize or justify one's right to be in the institution, which as the participant states, is exhausting, debilitating, and damaging. The participant is well aware that the infantilization that she experiences is the outcome of discrimination, although she is unable to 'prove' it. The effects of this are such that she is made to question if she is 'good enough.' As Ahmed suggests, 'the *encounter* with racism is experienced as the intimate labour of *countering* their idea of you' (2012: 160). Another participant further elaborated upon this, stating:

> I think self-doubt is always there when it comes to issues like racism, and that's why I always value colleagues of colour at other institutions that I

can call and say this or that happened. Sometimes it takes others to point out that something is unbelievably racist, and that self-doubt, sadly, I think is always there. It's self-doubt that allows racism and white supremacy to maintain itself because it knows that you always have that doubt, as a consequence they have a 'get out' – so the rude tone in the email has nothing to do with race, even though you know it does. It's the accumulation of these things on an individual level, and you start to learn that race does play a factor. (Interview 12)

In this response, we see the strain that self-doubt so often produces. The respondent speaks of seeking advice from external racially marked academics to 'verify' that what he has encountered is indeed racism. He also points to the way in which this is characteristic of how institutional racism in the university works, that is, its subtleties are as such that it provokes uncertainty and hesitation within the subjected. The challenge lies in being able to evidence, prove, or substantiate racism particularly when it occurs through slights, a look, or a tone; Bonilla-Silva's 'smiling face discrimination' springs to mind here. The accumulation that the respondent refers to is also demonstrative of the ways in which racially marked academics have to endure, or as Shirley Anne Tate (2012) describes, 'sup up' these practices of racism and exclusion on a long-term basis.

Notions of over-sensitivity or misinterpretation also contribute to emotional stress, as one participant said:

I think by the very nature of the way the university operates you're unsure of whether you're being oversensitive or if you've misinterpreted racism. I think often it comes in such subtle ways where you think you're reading too much into it. (Interview 16)

This was further explained by another interviewee who stated:

There is this sense of paranoia, like am I being sensitive? Am I just using the so-called 'race card' to legitimize the way I'm feeling? This constantly plays on my mind. And partially it makes me feel like is it my fault? There's a part of me that blames myself. (Interview 4)

The respondent expresses feelings of paranoia and questions whether he is using the 'race card' or being 'overly sensitive' (Sian 2017: 6). The charge of playing the 'race card' is a common dread, and somewhat irritation, that many people of colour have had to endure for decades. Notions that people of colour somehow play the 'race card' are constitutive of a discourse of convenience that serves whiteness. That is, it conveniently individualizes racism, it conveniently erases violent racial histories, and it conveniently shuts down any conversation on race. As Christopher J. Gilbert and Jonathan P. Rossing point out, 'efforts to dismiss race through recriminating charges of "playing the race card"' reinscribe a more problematic, inveterate racial consciousness" (2013: 93). The trope of the 'race card' is thus an easy route into legitimizing whiteness through the denial of the significance of race.

The feelings of doubt held by the respondent as to whether or not he is guilty of playing the 'race card' are understandable, particularly against the backdrop of a white academic environment. Because the kind of racism operating in universities is so subtle in nature and less easy to detect, the racially marked body is made to question their own actions and practices, rather than the other way round (Essed 1991; Sian 2017: 7). Anderson J. Franklin, Nancy Boyd-Franklin, and Shalonda Kelly warn that a key problem linked to microaggressions is the internalization of racism, whereby people of colour start to believe in their own subordination and accept negative attitudes (2006: 18; Sian 2017: 7). In this example, the respondent indicates elements of internalization through the questioning, self-doubting, and self-blaming of himself. The psychological trauma linked to racism as alluded to by my respondents develops from the sustained stress, emotional abuse, and self-doubt provoked by institutional racism (Franklin et al. 2006: 13; Sian 2017: 7). Another respondent further evoked the slow suffering of racism:

> I'm just paranoid, it's very hard for me to build trust with white colleagues. It's extremely difficult. It's a question of perseverance- of mental and physical perseverance. It is making me a worse person but I've got to be pragmatic in that space. You fall most when your levels of expectation are higher, so when you're in a HE environment you often think these

people are smart, intelligent people, they studied this stuff and they get it –
but then time and time again those people let you down and it destroys
you. (Interview 9)

The effects of racism in the university are telling. The respondent is on
what Ahmed describes as, 'perpetual guard' (2012: 161), that is, not
only having to be ready to defend himself, but also having to be prepared in order to protect himself. Like the previous interviewees, he
similarly speaks of paranoia, but also of physical and emotional perseverance to ensure that his colleagues and the environment itself does not
destroy him. This is the clear-cut violence of racism in British universities. It has been demoralizing, depressing, and distressing to go through
reams of transcripts of talented racially marked academics, and read
and revisit the mental trauma and physical pain that they have had to
endure while working in higher education. As racially marked academics we know all too well that the university is a far cry away from the
'safe space' that it claims to be. The academy for racially marked academics, is an undeniably harmful environment. It damages our confidence, it damages our sense of worth, and it damages our health.

Pub Culture: 'Whites Only' Social Spaces

Exclusionary practices of racism affecting racially marked academics travel beyond the institution. These are perhaps even more so pronounced in informal social settings, where colleagues often meet up to
relax, unwind, and network. What I'm referring to specifically here is
white, male, academic pub culture. Women in general have often been
constrained in large areas of public life, which represents a space typically dominated by (white) men. Traditionally women have tended to
be over-represented in the private sphere, whereas men have continued
to occupy the public sphere. Pubs, clubs, and bars have long represented
male preserves and have historically (and presently) posed a threat to
women. For example, despite recent moves to reduce male-dominated
drinking establishments through more choice and 'female-friendly'
spaces, research has shown that approximately two-thirds of women

encounter sexual harassment on nights out (Chatterton and Holland 2002: 102). Although it remains significantly important to point to these patriarchal constraints, research appears to have paid less attention to these spaces as being racially coded and dominated by whiteness.

Literature has conventionally focused upon the idea of 'no go areas' for whites, in what have been reductively considered as, 'black enclaves,' however 'white enclaves' or 'no go areas' for people of colour—as perhaps best symbolized by the British pub—have failed to warrant the same level of examination or analysis. Without over-simplifying, pubs have traditionally been spaces inhabited by British white males (ibid.; Long et al. 2014: 1790). Increasingly, with the development of the night-time economy combined with new forms of cosmopolitan urbanism, pubs have, for the most part, changed and adapted to shifting cultural landscapes to meet new demands (Chatterton and Holland 2002). However, despite these market-driven attempts to reimagine the traditional pub, as well as public order interventions around 'thug pubs' (ibid.: 105), the vast majority of pubs still continue to signify sites of exclusion in two key ways. Firstly, many BME populations fear that they will experience forms of violent racism. Secondly, the activity itself of 'going to the pub' is bound up with cultural norms of quintessential (white) Britishness, which some ethnic and racial groups cannot relate to in the same sort of way.

My participants spoke of their discomfort around the dominance of academic pub culture, which was felt to both signal their difference, and systematically exclude them from certain networks and opportunities. This was particularly felt by my Muslim respondents, however was by no means exclusive to them, as we will go onto to see racially marked female academics also experienced a clear sense of uneasiness. For many Muslim academics it was felt that such social events alienated them, as one participant suggested, these events often operate on a one-way basis that fails to consider non-drinkers, who in order to be included are expected to 'play their part' despite their non-drinking:

I've always tried my best to socialize with my colleagues, and a lot of that takes place around spaces in which alcohol is the central defining feature. I've never had a problem with socializing in such spaces, but I constantly feel like the pressure is on me to be a particular way. I don't even drink alcohol but I'm always having to be the one who has to integrate, whereas the spaces I may go to eat, or the spaces that I hang out in, would be places where my colleagues would never even dream about coming in order to make me feel at home. I feel like I have to juggle between being a certain way in order to acquire social upward mobility, and being myself. Why do I always have to do certain things? Why can't they arrange certain events that cater for everyone? I can't eat the meat, I can't drink the alcohol; I constantly feel out of place as a result of it. (Interview 4)

The sense of feeling out of place in particular social settings was commented upon across my interviews. Another key concern for my respondents was that by not participating within these events, they felt that they were more likely to miss out on particular opportunities, as one respondent said:

Pretty much all of our social events will be alcohol-centric, and so you may or may not choose to participate in them, but as you go on, if you don't drink it gets tedious, you know those are the kinds of spaces where often opportunities come up, you know people having conversations, where it's like 'oh this is going on, would you be interested in being involved?' So if you don't participate you're less likely to be included in things. (Interview 3)

The sense of exclusion experienced as a result of 'white academic networks,' and the negative impact that this was felt to have on career advancement and prospects, was also commented upon by the next interviewee who stated that:

Certain cliques of colleagues get more opportunities. I'm not part of the right networks; I'm Muslim, I don't drink or participate in that pub culture where we know a lot of decisions are made – where someone gets an arm round the shoulder and told that they're next in terms of promotion. So I face those exclusions. At university you need to be part of these networks, and at my university it's about being part of the old white boys network, where decisions are made in pubs, or somebody has been appointed to quite a prestigious role and you're like, 'I didn't see that advertised!' (Interview 13)

This was picked up by another participant who said:

> In my experience at the universities that I have worked at, I have found that colleagues always have to go immediately to the pub; this was a big issue for me. There was a pressure for me to move in that direction, but I resisted it and I made it clear that it wasn't working for me. I said we need to meet in a different forum, and there was no attempt at all to accommodate these other needs. And you suffer as a result. This extends beyond the institution, it happens at conferences and events, and the pub is where 'real things' happen, like networking, advancement and opportunities and so on. I often see those involved in this culture suddenly having opportunities opened to them, and I used to think where did this get discussed? Then it's clear it was discussed the other night in the pub. (Interview 19)

As previously mentioned, feelings of being disregarded in the social sense were not confined to only Muslim staff members. Racially marked female academics also expressed concerns that departmental social activities were not accommodating, and catered only for particular male white networks. This functioned to make my participants feel a greater sense of marginalization and non-belonging, for example:

> I don't feel like I've fitted in, particularly in a social sense, it's often been a group of white men who will go for a drink together. Here you get the feeling both the social and the academic is coming together, and it has worked to make me feel excluded. Things very much come out of these social groupings - so opportunities to be involved in events, publishing, or research bids. It's been up to me to actively invite myself to these spaces. (Interview 16)

Similarly, another respondent pointed out that:

> You're the last to know, you feel like you're always the last to know about things that affect you, the department or students. And part of it is because of the fact that you're not at the pub later on – so the actual networking and the building of social capital that happens usually within white male networks – we're not involved in that, and how it manifests itself. (Interview 20)

She goes onto say:

> On rare occasions I might go along, but you need to have the energy to prepare yourself mentally to go to those places, because it's not only about being in that space with academics, it's also the other people in the pub, and where the pub is. There are certain pubs attached to certain universities where the faculty would go and the faculty are known, so if you were to go to that place without the old guard, you're interrogated. Even if you do go along with them I feel like you can't relax into the scene, it just feels like an old, white, traditional English setting, and you try and engage as much as you can but it's just not designed for you and you know it. So it reinforces the fact that academic culture was not designed with you in mind- at all. (Interview 20)

Here the respondent really captures the psychological damage involved in entering pubs with her white colleagues, whereby not only does she have to carefully negotiate her performance with them, but also within the space itself. She makes us aware that she has to be on alert in relation to other individuals in the pub as well as considering the location of the pub, in other words, weighing up whether or not it is a 'safe space' for her body to be within. The respondent similarly speaks of 'white networks' and the consequences that often occur if one represents a 'newcomer' to that already long established white, male academic grouping. The harmful nature of the pub space is clearly expressed by the respondent who feels that she cannot relax because the architecture, and the design of the setting, is dictated by exclusionary white, British codes. She goes onto argue that as a result of such processes it becomes clear that academic culture fails to consider the needs of racially marked academics, which both reflects and reproduces the broader structural dynamics of the university, i.e. Whiteness/exclusion. This feeling was also expressed by another female respondent who said:

> If your difference is that you don't drink, the department is not able to embrace that, and say, 'you know what why don't we go to a café, or go bowling?' I don't fucking know but somewhere that everybody, all members of staff can feel comfortable. (Interview 1)

The responses have demonstrated the way in which exclusionary practices of racism are not simply confined to departmental or faculty level politics. Rather, they also extend into the social academic setting, which for the most part, involves participating within a narrow, provincial, white pub culture. This social space works to further marginalize, undervalue, and undermine racially marked academics on a number of different levels. Firstly it is composed of an exclusive network that appears off-bounds, and highly inaccessible, for racially marked academics to penetrate or participate within, that is, it is a predominantly small, tight-knit network, of white (senior) male staff members. Secondly, the fact that the large majority of social activities take place within pubs, or other drinking establishments, immediately signals to racially marked academics, from particular ethnic and religious backgrounds, that they are not welcome. Third, the actual environment of the white British pub can often provoke fear and discomfort for racially marked academics due to associated issues around racism, harassment and violence, i.e. it does not always represent a safe or welcoming space. Together these factors illustrate quite clearly that the general culture of the university is one that accommodates only for whiteness, thus failing miserably to cater for the different, wider needs of all its staff members. Such failure is representative of the prevalence of institutional racism in British universities, and contributes to the ongoing exclusion of racially marked academics, by sending them the message that they do not belong, both in the professional and social sense.

Conclusion

This chapter has examined the performance of everyday racism operating in British universities. It has documented countless daily interactions of racism experienced by racially marked academics, and in doing so, it has illustrated that such encounters are not merely the product of a few 'bad apples.' What we have seen throughout this chapter are not just a small number of isolated experiences of racism, but rather a catalogue of widespread incidents that are all similar in nature. This demonstrates the way in which racial microaggressions intertwine with institutional racism and white privilege to systematically exclude racially marked academics. There is a clear sense of a shared familiarity across the responses which points to the prevalence of racism in the academy. We have unravelled the processes by which racially marked academics are located on the margins through a range of subtle performances and practices, that undermine and undervalue them on a daily basis, as hooks describes, 'to be in the margin is to be part of the whole but outside the main body' (1989: 20). The locating of our bodies on the outside has taken shape through liberal enunciations, whereby the racism experienced by my respondents is not overt, but rather operates through differential treatment.

We also went onto analyse the various processes of othering that racially marked academics encounter and the gendered racism underpinning particular classifications such as, 'troublemaker' or 'exotic.' We saw the manifestation of the interplay between hyper-visibility and invisibility that worked to both exceptionalize and dismiss racially marked academics, often simultaneously, and considered the emotional and psychological effects of such processes. Finally, the chapter examined how these practices also operated in a social sense to further marginalize racially marked academics.

Critics may argue that the encounters described throughout this chapter are simply 'vague' or 'subjective' and therefore 'unreliable,' as Sue et al. point out, often is the case that, 'covert forms of racism are not as valid or as important as racist events that can be quantified and "proven"' (Sue et al. 2007: 283). However, it is precisely this kind of critique that encourages those within these institutions to 'turn a blind eye' to their own practices of, and complicity with, racism (ibid.). The downplaying of these incidents, due to their less obvious nature, is to legitimize harmful, hegemonic systems of whiteness. Furthermore, the idea that racial microaggressions are somehow 'less damaging' is to also fall into the trap of reducing the effects and the impact that they have upon racially marked academics. It is precisely because racial microaggressions in the university space operate in such a covert manner that a close examination remains necessary. Sue et al. go onto argue that, 'without documentation and analysis to help better understand microaggressions, the threats that they pose and the assaults that they justify can be easily ignored or downplayed' (ibid.). This chapter has set out to foreground microaggressions and takes seriously the effects that they have upon racially marked academics. By placing considerable attention upon these interactions, I have sought to critically understand the experiences within broader frameworks of institutional racism, post-raciality and whiteness. This has allowed an analysis to form that understands everyday racism not simply as an individual phenomenon, but rather as a multifaceted process that sits within a wider structural context.

Notes

1. Get Out. (2017). Universal Pictures: USA.
2. This will be examined further in Chapter 5.
3. For further elaboration of the interplay between ethnic marking and unmarking see, Hesse and Sayyid (2006) 'The Postcolonial Political and the Immigrant Imaginary', p. 23.
4. See Fanon (1986) *Black Skin White Masks*, p. 82.

References

Ahmed, S. (2004). Affective Economies. *Social Text, 79, 22*(2), 117–139.
Ahmed, S. (2007). A Phenomenology of Whiteness. *Feminist Theory, 8*(2), 149–168.
Ahmed, S. (2012). *On Being Included: Racism and Diversity in Institutional Life*. Durham: Duke University Press.
Bakare, L. (2017, February 28). Get Out: The Film That Dares to Reveal the Horror of Liberal Racism in America. *The Guardian*. https://www.theguardian.com/film/2017/feb/28/get-out-box-office-jordan-peele.
Bhopal, K. (2016). *The Experiences of Black and Minority Ethnic Academics: A Comparative Study of the Unequal Academy*. London: Routledge.
Bonilla-Silva, E. (2003). *Racism Without Racists: Color-Blind Racism and the Persistence of Racial Inequality in the United States*. Lanham, MD: Rowman & Littlefield.

Chatterton, P., & Hollands, R. (2002). Theorising Urban Playscapes: Producing, Regulating and Consuming Youthful Nightlife City Spaces. *Urban Studies, 39*(1), 65–116.

Coleman, R., & McCahill, M. (2011). *Surveillance and Crime*. London: Sage.

Davis, A. (2003). *Are Prisons Obsolete?*. New York: Seven Stories Press.

Essed, P. (1991). *Understanding Everyday Racism: An Interdisciplinary Theory*. Newbury Park: Sage.

Fanon, F. (1986). *Black Skin White Masks*. London: Pluto Press.

Fitzgibbon, D. (2007). Institutional Racism, Pre-Emptive Criminalisation and Risk Analysis. *The Howard Journal, 46*(2), 128–144.

Franklin, A. J. (1999). Invisibility Syndrome and Racial Identity Development in Psychotherapy and Counseling African American Men. *The Counseling Psychologist, 27*(6), 761–793.

Franklin, A. J., Boyd-Franklin, N., & Kelly, S. (2006). Racism and Invisibility. *Journal of Emotional Abuse, 6*(2–3), 9–30.

Gallini, C. (1996). Mass Exoticisms. In I. Chambers & L. Curti (Eds.), *The Postcolonial Question: Common Skies, Divided Horizons* (pp. 212–220). London: Routledge.

Garner, S. (2010). *Racisms: An Introduction*. London: Sage.

Get Out. (2017). Universal Pictures: USA.

Gilbert, C., & Rossing, J. (2013). Trumping Tropes with Joke(r)s: The Daily Show "Plays the Race Card". *Western Journal of Communication, 77*(1), 92–111.

Goldberg, D. (2013). The Post-racial Contemporary. In N. Kapoor, V. Kalra, & J. Rhodes (Eds.), *The State of Race* (pp. 15–30). Houndmills: Palgrave.

Hall, C. (2014). Catherine Hall. In K. Sian (Ed.), *Conversations in Postcolonial Thought* (pp. 49–61). New York: Palgrave.

Hall, S. et al. (2013). *Policing the Crisis: Mugging, the State and Law and Order* (2nd ed.). London: Palgrave Macmillan.

Hesse, B. (2004). Discourse on Institutional Racism: The Genealogy of a Concept. In I. Law, D. Phillips, & L. Turney (Eds.), *Institutional Racism in Higher Education* (pp. 131–145). Staffordshire: Trentham Books.

Hesse, B., & Sayyid, S. (2006). The Postcolonial Political and the Immigrant Imaginary. In N. Ali, V. Kalra, & S. Sayyid (Eds.), *A Postcolonial People: South Asians in Britain* (pp. 13–31). London: Hurst and Company.

Hill-Collins, P. (1986). Learning from the Outsider Within: The Sociological Significance of Black Feminist Thought. *Social Problems, 33*(6), S14–S32.

hooks, b. (1989). Choosing the Margin as a Space of Racial Openness. *The Journal of Cinema and Media, 36*, 15–23.

Lander, V., & Santoro, N. (2017). Invisible and Hypervisible Academics: The Experiences of Black and Minority Ethnic Teacher Educators. *Teaching in Higher Education, 22*(8), 1008–1021.

Long, J., Hylton, K., & Spacklen, K. (2014). Whiteness, Blackness and Settlement: Leisure and the Integration of New Migrants. *Journal of Ethnic and Migration Studies, 40*(11), 1779–1797.

Madriz, E. (1997). Images of Criminals and Victims: A Study on Women's Fear and Social Control. *Gender and Society, 11*(3), 342–356.

Mirza, H. (2006). Transcendence Over Diversity: Black Women in the Academy. *Policy Futures in Education, 4*(2), 101–113.

Mohanty, C. (1988). Under Western Eyes: Feminist Scholarship and Colonial Discourses. *Feminist Review, 30,* 61–88.

Okazaki, S. (2009). Impact of Racism on Ethnic Minority Mental Health. *Social Issues, Association for Psychological Science, 4*(1), 103–107.

Patel, T. (2017). *Race and Society*. London: Sage.

Purwar, N. (2004). Fish In and Out of Water: A Theoretical Framework for Race and the Space of Academia. In I. Law, D. Phillips, & L. Turney (Eds.), *Institutional Racism in Higher Education* (pp. 49–58). Staffordshire: Trentham Books.

Reid, L., & Birchard, K. (2010). The People Doth Protest Too Much: Explaining Away Subtle Racism. *Journal of Language and Social Psychology, 29*(4), 478–490.

Said, E. (1978). *Orientalism*. London: Penguin Books.

Sian, K. (2017). Being Black in a White World: Understanding Racism in British Universities. *International Journal on Collective Identity Research, 176*(2), 1–26.

Sian, K., Law, I., & Sayyid, B. (2013). *Racism, Governance and Public Policy: Beyond Human Rights*. London: Routledge.

Sue, D. et al. (2007). Racial Microaggressions in Everyday Life: Implications for Clinical Practice. *American Psychologist, 62*(4), 271–286.

Tate, S. A. (2012). "Supping it": Racial Affective Economies and the Epistemology of Ignorance. In M. Christian (Ed.), *Integrated But Unequal: Black Faculty in Predominantly White Spaces*. Trenton, NJ: Africa World Press.

Tyrer, D. (2013). *The Politics of Islamophobia: Race, Power and Fantasy*. London: Pluto Press.

Ware, V. (1996). Defining Forces: "Race", Gender and Memories of Empire. In I. Chambers & L. Curti (Eds.), *The Postcolonial Question: Common Skies, Divided Horizons* (pp. 142–156). London: Routledge.

Yancy, G. (2017). *On Race, 34 Conversations in a Time of Crisis*. New York: Oxford University Press.

Zamudio, M., & Rios, F. (2006). From Traditional to Liberal Racism: Living Racism in the Everyday. *Sociological Perspectives, 49*(4), 483–501.

4

Teaching Experiences

Introduction

The classroom setting is often thought to represent a 'safe space' that encourages critical learning, the exchange of ideas, and pedagogical tools to generate future knowledge (Sian 2017: 11). However, it would be naive to simply suggest that the classroom is free from antagonism, particularly because it sits within a broader university environment that is structured by institutional racism. It follows then that the classroom is not race-neutral, but rather it is entrenched 'in the political' and can therefore often pose a number of challenges for racially marked academics to negotiate (Chan et al. 2014: 3). That is, the classroom can become a key site in which white students may express feelings of guilt, confront their privilege, or challenge the authority of the educator; such dynamics can be seen to represent and reinforce the wider racist logics of the academy (ibid.; Sian 2017: 12).

In my own experiences I have found teaching in British universities difficult, challenging, and at times rewarding (Sian 2017: 12). When I first started out as a teaching assistant I remember leading a seminar class on racism and popular culture, and a white, middle class, male student put up his hand and smugly remarked, '*but everybody knows black*

© The Author(s) 2019
K. P. Sian, *Navigating Institutional Racism in British Universities*,
Mapping Global Racisms, https://doi.org/10.1007/978-3-030-14284-1_4

people have smaller brains than white people' (ibid.). I was shocked and dazed, my body froze as anger and rage filled my insides. Nonetheless, I continued with the class as the comment was immediately challenged by a female student of colour who appeared to feel the same way that I did (ibid.). I wanted to give her the space to critique him and it went on to provoke an important discussion whereby his white peers also went onto challenge his assertion (ibid.). The boy was left with a red face and he went on to apologize. I remember leaving the classroom and immediately running up the stairs to see my mentor, a person of colour (ibid.). As I started to tell him what had happened I broke down and cried. From that day on I was fortunate to have his guidance, which went onto prepare me with the tools to deal with situations of this nature (ibid.). I know I was one of the lucky ones, as I had a mentor who was able to support me and help me to develop the confidence to productively challenge racism in such settings… others however, as we will go onto see, have not been as fortunate.

Whitelash

Whiteness and white privilege are staple features of the student body across universities in Britain (Sian 2017: 12). These discourses are reinforced by the under-representation of students of colour, for example in terms of student participation the Equality and Human Rights Commission (EHRC) Triennial Review (2010) reported that the number of BME students has increased from 13% of students in 1994/1995 to 23% in 2008/2009 (Runnymede Trust 2010: 2). Although this figure appears proportionate to their size in the young population, it is important to note that they are woefully under-represented in Russell Group institutions (Sian 2017: 12). For instance, evidence from the Runnymede Trust found that there are more students of Black Caribbean origin at London Metropolitan University than at all the Russell Group universities put together (Runnymede Trust 2010: 2). Against this landscape racism in the classroom (and beyond) is rarely, if at all, challenged by white faculty members, alas, that task is almost always left to racially marked academics.

For Adrienne Chan, Rita Dhamoon, and Lisa Moy, when racially marked academics do engage with difficult topics such as race and ethnicity, they are often required to take on certain forms of 'labour-intensive roles' including 'curator/choreographer of emotions,' 'tour guide,' 'puzzler,' 'instructor as book,' 's**t disturber/catalyst' (2014: 19). Their important study revealed that when teaching topics that disrupt hegemonic norms, the racially marked lecturer is often read as, 'not easy to get along with, as hostile and unhappy, as someone who is responsible for tensions and divisions in society, as someone who is not a real scholar but motivated by ideology' (ibid.: 15). Such experiences resonate with my respondents whose bodies came to frequently represent sites of suspicion, danger, or mockery, as a result they were often left fearful, unable in some cases to tackle the tensions that they encountered within the classroom (Sian 2017: 16). These acts of provocation experienced by my interviewees can be defined as whitelash, that is, backlash from white students who oppose learning about racism and thus refuse to acknowledge, recognize, and engage with it (Matias 2018: 10). As we will go onto see when such issues are discussed within the classroom setting, racially marked academics are confronted with a series of hostile responses.

Roxana Ng suggests that institutional racism (and sexism) have been normalized and naturalized to such an extent within the academy that they are closed from critique and reflection (1993: 191; Sian 2017: 13). She details her own experiences as a female racialized lecturer, and draws our attention to the challenges that she encountered in the classroom. Ng describes an incident whereby a student accused her of using the course to facilitate the development of her own 'political agenda,' he complained that he had been marginalized/oppressed as a white male, and in follow up meetings with administrative staff he stated that she was 'a woman out of control' (ibid.). My respondents recalled similar experiences voicing concerns around engaging with critical discussions and the whitelash that they encountered as a result, for example one participant said:

My experience of teaching is centred around being in a constant state of fear, especially when teaching in subject areas such as racism, Islamophobia, and so on. I feel under threat that one of my students is going to report me to a member of staff, and the university will take some kind of disciplinary action against me, for articulating a particular argument. Why should I have to feel this afraid about talking about racism or Islamophobia, or critiquing policy? Why should I be afraid to talk about this in my own class? (Interview 4)

He goes onto recall an encounter whereby a white male student directly challenged him in the lecture theatre. In this case not only was he expected to listen to the Islamophobic rantings of the student, but he was also required to defend his position (as well as the broader position of Islam), because as a Muslim man it was assumed by the student that he somehow represented the entire religion, as he describes:

> I've had one encounter with a white male undergraduate student, who challenged me on a series of issues when I explained the topic of political violence. He started to ask questions and make points that were Islamophobic. He was talking about child molestation by the Prophet Muhammad, how Islam had been a religion spread by the sword, how Muslims believed in female genital mutilation, and so on. I was constantly having to explain and defend a religion of over a billion people, because somehow in the eyes of the student, I was Islam; so I found that to be a really uncomfortable experience. (Interview 4)

This represents an explicit exercise in Islamophobia whereby the student seeks to undermine the authority of the lecturer through a string of provocative and pejorative statements (Sian 2017: 14). In this way we can see how violent forms of whiteness are performed and projected through Islamophobia as an attempt to reclaim the dominance of the classroom setting; in other words, what we see is a clear example of the playing out of power dynamics whereby the student is evidently threatened by the presence of a racially marked academic in a position of power (ibid.). Another respondent spoke of a similar experience:

> Some of my most troubling encounters have been with students. I was teaching my course related to issues of racism, crime and politics, and two white female mature students always challenged me. I think this relates to how they perceived me as a young brown academic. They'd interrupt

during the lecture and say things like they'd also encountered profiling so it wasn't just those from ethnic minority backgrounds. (Interview 13)

He goes onto say:

> One particular incident happened which was one of the most challenging things I've ever had to deal with, where one of these students used the word P*** in the middle of the class. She kept repeating the word, and it was difficult to deal with because she was supposedly making her point, rather than targeting it directly at someone. I didn't challenge it because I actually didn't know what to do, I didn't want to shut it down because I didn't want to be accused of being biased. These women constantly tried to challenge me, because I think they felt quite empowered to do so. They'd ask questions that would deliberately challenge. This made me really anxious because I was put under pressure. (Interview 13)

The extract demonstrates a strong sense of familiarity with the previous experience documented, whereby once again the participant had been subjected to Islamophobic comments and hostility in the middle of a lecture by two of his white students. The students are both female which takes us back to the previous chapter and the reinforcing of the notion that particularly white females appear to have a problem with men of colour in senior roles. It represents yet another example of white women attempting to domesticate racially marked male bodies in the academy. In this incident, we clearly see the way in which the respondent is met with antagonism and a strong sense of resentment. The Islamophobic use of the term P***, which is repeated on several occasions, operates to further undermine and humiliate my participant, who was left feeling uncomfortable and anxious by the experience. This is an explicit performance of gendered racism whereby the white female students are seeking to discipline his racially marked body. Depressingly these encounters were fairly common for my participants across a range of different universities, for example another participant said:

> I really feel like I'm a black man stood at the front of the room. I teach on race and I can see that there's an undertone of white backlash from the students, I can see the anger at times, possibly shame and guilt at

times, but it's all very uncomfortable. You sense that they would prefer white tutors stood in front of them talking about exactly the same thing, and I suspect it would go down a lot better. I feel very black in this context, to the point of where the pressure on me to get it right is immense. I'm very confident about my knowledge, but when I'm teaching my undergrads I'm very conscious of being very clear in what I'm saying because if not, the hand goes straight up. Only recently this happened to me in a class I was teaching. I'd opened the lecture, and within a minute a student put up their hand and said, 'it's not only black people that have the experiences you're talking about.' So I had an immediate backlash. (Interview 10)

In this response, we see yet again the lecturer being interrupted during his class. There is a strong sense of white student entitlement, which clearly makes some of them feel powerful enough to disrupt the lecture setting. Furthermore it is interesting that in this encounter, as with the previous ones, the common complaint from white students is that white people also experience what people of colour experience, i.e. it isn't just people of colour who are affected by processes and practices of racism. We know all too well that some white people are keen to get on the defensive about issues concerning race/ethnicity, and some like to claim that in fact they are the largest victims of racism.[1] The inability of these students to critically reflect upon their own histories, practices, and structures of oppression is symptomatic of white privilege, white entitlement, and white guilt. All these features fuse together in a melodramatic display of whitelash, which sees the all too common spewing out of racist bile because they feel that their dominant position is under threat by racially marked bodies in the academy. This attempt to undermine and essentially bully racially marked academics was further illustrated by another respondent who said:

Students snigger, they roll their eyes, a number of them walk out and it happens all the time. So I've had to try and deal with this, because it's made me very uncomfortable. I start sweating, I start rushing my material, and I just want to get it over with because it's such a horrible experience. They make out over and over again that I don't know what I'm talking about, or that I'm biased and it makes me extremely uncomfortable – and these are 18 year olds for God's sake that are making me feel like that! (Interview 9)

The next participant also raised this sense of feeling resented, and recalled an incident in which a white student directly questioned her legitimacy:

I remember one time I was teaching a grammar class and I came in early to set up the classroom. There were two Indian students in the front of the room and one British white girl. So the two Indian students saw me and were like, 'oh where are you from, it's really cool that you're teaching this class', so I told them my parents were from India, but that I was from the USA… and this white British girl from the other side of the room smugly said 'so how are you teaching this class?' I was just so shocked and lost for words, I felt so deeply uncomfortable about it. (Interview 6)

The damaging psychological, emotional, and physical effects of whitelash are clear from my respondents. Racially marked academics have to endure, or be prepared for, being subjected to abuse and hostility from white students. All of my participants shared the common feeling of being uncomfortable when these confrontations occur, and the sense of isolation felt was quite apparent. The racial harassment that they have experienced in the classroom has clearly impacted upon their well-being, confidence, and self-esteem, we will come back to this later on in the chapter. My participants also spoke of the extra burden attached to teaching courses related to critical race issues, for example:

I think teaching race carries with it an extra burden, because you're not only teaching students about these issues, but also you're teaching them life skills. I've found students like to correct the way I'm speaking, or interrupt me and so on. They like to test my credibility, and ask inappropriate questions to almost test my ability. They try to slip you up and try to talk over you. I over prepare because when they ask me something, I don't want them to think I don't know something, when I do. (Interview 11)

The respondent feels like her authority is constantly being tested by her white students, which is both reflective of the racial and gendered dynamic of the classroom setting, as well as the nature of the content discussed which she suspects will be open to more questioning, thus over-prepares as a result. Philomena Essed argues that formal spaces of education have failed to expose students to critical ideas on race and racism (2000: 900), as a result, racially marked academics are all too often left unsupported to deal with the strains and the consequences attached to teaching these areas, as one participant commented:

> I think sometimes you do have to shut down the debate because it's not productive because it's so problematic. I do feel like there's an additional burden because a lot of other teachers don't care, or don't have the tools, or they don't go out of their way to get those tools to unpack racism, so it's always left to us. (Interview 2)

Another interviewee also went onto express that racially marked academics are often situated and implicated within these debates as they often represent their everyday realities and lived experiences, she says:

> It's difficult to deliver politically charged content, because we are also positioned within that politically. We are deeply involved in these issues because they form our realities. (Interview 20)

Chan et al. argue that the assumptions and expectations that racially marked academics are both willing and equipped to teach sensitive areas, that are related to complex emotions and tensions—where there is the real possibility of epistemic violence—is another, exploitative form of labour that we are required to carry out in the academy (2014: 18). They also go onto suggest that challenging white privilege is often opposed by students leading to tension, as well as apprehension within the educators themselves (ibid.: 18), much of this dynamic we have already seen being played out in my interviews. Similarly, Shirin Housee argues that teaching issues around race and racism often 'require checks and balances that are unnecessary in other subjects' (2008: 427), due to the relations of power operating at the interpersonal and political level.

The hostility that my participants have experienced can be seen as an explicit exercise in whitelash, whereby the students actively seek to undermine racially marked academics due to a combination of resentment, guilt, and white fragility (Bailey 2017: 61). The presence of racially marked academics in the teaching space disrupts the 'protective' environment that many white students demand and expect (ibid.). This environment is structured by 'racial comfort' and shields them from having to confront difficult issues that question their historical and contemporary worldview (ibid.). White resentment and whitelash, as we have clearly seen throughout this section, are therefore projected onto racially marked academics who are seen to be agitators and aggressors, rather than critical educators promoting rich, wider, analytical thought.

Dominant Perceptions: Credibility, Authority and Proficiency

As demonstrated by the previous responses racially marked academics often find that their credibility and authority is increasingly challenged, questioned, and undermined by white students in the teaching environment. There is a clear gendered dynamic to the racism at play in the classroom. We saw earlier how animosity from students tends to be more pronounced on the bodies of racially marked male academics, who are prone to experiencing a more direct tirade of abuse and insults. However for racially marked female academics, insults are less direct and more passive aggressive in an attempt to locate them as teachers that lack credibility. For example, Purwar argues that 'authority is seen to be especially misplaced when it is clearly vested in a woman of colour' (2004: 52), similarly Sylvia R. Lazos suggests that, 'both minorities and women are presumed to be incompetent as soon as they walk in the door' (2012a: 177). As we will go onto see such a positioning can leave racially marked women feeling powerless in the academy.

In my own experiences, I have found myself being mistaken for a student, subjected to hostility that appears to be based on the notion of perceived lack of authority (as racially marked and female), and being abruptly interrupted or spoken over (Sian 2017: 15). This demonstrates the way in which students continue to underestimate and undervalue the position, qualifications, and skills of racialized (particularly female) academics. Gendered and racist power relations therefore significantly condition how students perceive formal authority; these relations combine to essentially 'disempower' racialized teachers (Ng 1993: 190). From my interview responses racially marked female academics tended to express feelings of being infantilized by the white student body, whereby their physical appearance was often subjected to scrutiny, for example:

> I don't know what part of me makes them behave to me or speak to me in a certain way, it's the whole package; it is my height, my voice, I look very young, I have really long hair so I'm hyper-feminine and very exotic. So I on purpose don't wear too many colours when I teach, because I don't want them to see me as less. (Interview 2)

Lazos argues that when women are in roles and jobs that are typically viewed or coded as male they will encounter stereotypical perceptions that, 'they are not competent, authoritative, or charismatic leaders' (2012a: 176), and are likely to receive backlash when they fail to conform to student stereotypes. This can be seen being reflected in the following response:

> Because I wear Asian dress I have felt that students would often look me up and down; the initial reaction is that students don't expect me to be doing the role that I do. So it's always this idea that I lack credibility, I think many of the students come with a lot of stereotypes, which is natural. With time, I think teaching has become easier. (Interview 11)

My male respondents were also cognizant of the gender dynamic at play and were sympathetic to the extra challenges that racially marked female academics encounter, for example:

> I think there are certain privileges to being a man of colour teaching, rather than a woman of colour. The students give me a little bit more respect without it being earned. I feel like I can walk into a classroom and

students are more ready to assume that I know what I'm talking about. I think being a man gives me a bit more privilege. (Interview 12)

The double exclusion that racially marked female academics experience, through structural forms of racism and patriarchy, serves to make them more exposed and vulnerable to hostility from students (Sian 2017: 14). For example, in her research on female academics of colour, Linda Trinh Vo details how she had to psychologically prepare herself for antagonistic teaching environments (2012: 102–103; Sian 2017: 15). She is aware that for many of her students she was likely to have been the first racially marked person that they had encountered, as such they were hostile about not only being taught by a female in a position of seniority, but also by someone who they would regard as 'foreign' (ibid.). This was also picked up in an incident experienced by one of my respondents who recalled:

For many first years you're sometimes their first black or brown experience (laughs). I took over a seminar once, and a student just sat and stared at me the whole time, I don't know if that's because I'm a woman, or because I'm black, or both – but it's clear I'm not their typical exposure in these spaces. I was just shell-shocked; I couldn't break the spell, the student literally just stared at me the whole time (laughs). It's so interesting. In my teaching experience, I've noticed I am the last thing students expect, the last thing. And when your breath of knowledge is demonstrated, which in our cases it usually is because we have to know everything and over prepare – they're taken aback. And that exposure is a good thing, but it's unfortunate that it's 2018 and I'm their first experience. (Interview 20)

This example takes us back to earlier discussions raised in the previous chapter around hyper-visibility. Here we see clearly the way in which the respondent is marked out by her blackness, and the sense of fascination and bewilderment such blackness provokes in white students, who it seems can only mindlessly stare and gawp at her. This deeply problematic response is indicative of not only their lack of exposure to people of colour, but also of the failings of the university in successfully

promoting, encouraging, and embedding diversity to ensure that difference is not such a rare occurrence.

The feeling around the need to over-prepare for classes was a key
issue that all my respondents addressed due to the pressure of a racist
environment that demands they prove their competence (Harlow 2003:
355). They all felt that they needed to be 'extra-equipped' in terms of
knowledge and materials to 'prove' their legitimacy and authority, as
one female stated:

> I definitely over-prepare, I spend ages and ages, because I don't want to
> look like I don't know what I'm talking about, I really worry about look-
> ing like I don't know what I'm talking about. (Interview 16)

For racially marked male academics there was a stronger sense that students tended to treat them more as friends. This comportment however
is also another way in which they are seen to lack authority compared to
their white peers:

> Students will often call me mate, but I know a white middle-aged man is
> never going to be called that. Partly that's to do with age, partly race, and
> partly the way I present myself. I know I'm often framed as being quite
> cool, but that's just from being a black mixed raced man, in some ways
> cool is good, but cool is also not incredibly academic or intellectual- so
> students will see me as someone who knows what I'm talking about but
> perhaps more from experience or being an activist, rather than someone
> whose knowledge is based on intellectual rigor. (Interview 12)

It is important to note here that the 'coolness' attached to blackness was
not male-specific as a female academic of colour also experienced similar
framings:

> In my experience - part of which I think has to do with hip-hop or black
> culture – I've noticed that a lot of students think I'm cool, its like they
> want to get on my good side. I've got an element of 'street cred' so they
> want to be my friend. Because of the idealization of black culture, I feel
> I am insulated from rude comments. The stereotypes of hip-hop, and so
> on, almost protect me from offensive behaviour from students, but then

that also means that I'm always read through this lens rather than that of an academic. (Interview 20)

A male academic of colour went onto further comment upon the informal dynamic at play with his students, which he suspected was racialized:

> I do feel a sense that students feel way too comfortable in seminar settings, and sometimes I think what's the causality of that? Is it the student or is it the dynamic with me being a junior person of colour? Do I encourage it, or do they start it? I don't know if the same would happen to a white colleague. (Interview 17)

The idea of not fitting into the 'traditional' lecturer profile was picked up by another respondent, who similarly felt that as a result he was more likely to be seen to lack credibility and face more challenges from his students:

> I always want to command the classroom and command respect. I do feel like I don't fit the traditional 'look' of a lecturer and that to students makes you appear less credible. I feel like you always have to be prepared for students to undermine your credibility or push your buttons. There's always a sense of dread there. It makes me second-guess myself. My lectures, I believe are rigorous, but I do have to constantly think about keeping students on side. (Interview 13)

The next respondent talks of the familiar assumption often placed on racially marked academics that they are not lecturers. This is a common perception that most racially marked academics face; as a result we are often tasked with the extra labour of proving our legitimacy:

> Many students sometimes assume I'm not a lecturer. And I sense that this is certainly racialized. You have to prove yourself and win that status. (Interview 18)

The notion of having to 'prove' oneself was an experience that came up time and time again across my interviews. We see the insidious workings of racism at play, whereby racially marked academics have to almost always go the extra mile to demonstrate their capacities and capabilities which are continually questioned by white students:

> I have felt a number of times that what I say is questioned and my integrity is questioned. Student's almost don't believe me, where as when white colleagues speak its insightful, it's gospel. (Interview 9)

Another respondent said:

> You're not only delivering content, you're also having to prove yourself as a legitimate person, because sometimes students feel like you shouldn't be teaching them. (Interview 20)

This again works to produce the haunting shadow of self-doubt and having to constantly prove or justify oneself as being a legitimate or deserving body within the teaching space. This is further complicated if the academic of colour is seen to have a 'foreign' accent which can further undermine credibility, as one participant noted:

> I can tell from observations in the classroom that if you have a strong Western European accent students think it's very cosmopolitan, but if it's an East Asian member of staff for example - even though they speak perfect English - they will say they can't understand, which is interesting. Those outside Western Europe are always seen to be difficult to understand. Their accent is picked up even if they speak good English. And this goes onto undermine their credibility as the knowledge they bring is often not taken seriously by students. (Interview 15)

Recent research has gone onto support this claim revealing that home students are less likely to trust lecturers with 'foreign' accents. It was reported that students do not take lecturers 'seriously' whose first language is not English, and are seen to be less credible compared to native speakers (Matthews, 15 November 2017: *Times Higher Education*).[2] We can see quite clearly the various challenges that racially marked academics face within the teaching environment. There are a number of racialized and gendered assumptions that students frequently attach to racially marked academics, which operate to undermine their authority.

This section has identified the effects of such damaging perceptions and stereotypes held by white students.

My interview data supports the extensive research existing in this area which has demonstrated time and time again the same patterns and same sets of issues at play. For example twenty years ago Katherine Grace Hendrix conducted an important study revealing that 'the competence of black professors was more likely to be questioned' (1998: 758). Similarly, research by Roxanna Harlow found that the lived reality for racialized academics is that, 'there will always be students who question their competency, credentials, and ability to teach and assess students' work' (2003: 362). From the way that they look, to the way that they speak, racially marked academics have to undergo a series of denunciations whereby they are subjected to a range of reductive, racist assumptions and attitudes, that invalidate both their position and capabilities within the academy.

Student Evaluations

Student evaluations are generally deemed useful for administrators and managers serving as a reliable tool to measure and monitor levels of positive and negative feedback (Lazos 2012a: 167). British universities often rely on student evaluations which feed into wider measurement indicators of 'excellence,' such as the Teaching Excellence Framework (TEF) and the National Student Survey (NSS).[3] Student evaluations can also be important in terms of determining promotions and career progression (Reid 2010: 137). However, they have also come under considerable critique over the years, largely around issues of ambiguity and subjectivity, making it often difficult to decipher what is actually being measured or indeed judged (Lazos 2012a: 165). Research has shown that student evaluations systematically generate low ratings for racially marked academics, (especially females). Student evaluations are therefore particularly dangerous for these groups as they are more vulnerable to unconscious bias from students, whose expectations are often rooted within racial and gendered stereotypes (ibid.: 166; Reid 2010: 147). As we have seen throughout this chapter, when racially marked academics do critically engage with 'difficult content' they are more than often accused of being bias, sensitive, angry, or turning everything back to the question of race (Sian 2017: 12). Such disgruntles are subsequently documented in their end of term evaluations whereby the sense of white resentment can often be explicit (Chan et al. 2014: 2). My interviewees revealed such concerns:

> Once I had really bad feedback because I called a student out on something that he said about Japanese Geishas being 'prostitutes,' I just didn't like where the conversation was going and it was getting more and more racialized and I said that's enough. So I got really bad feedback because I shut down the debate. (Interview 2)

The following response shows the way in which another participant was particularly vulnerable to 'verbal violence' from his students (Lazos 2012b: 466), to the extent at which he went on to receive a long critical email from one of them:

> The students often complain about me or give me bad feedback. I once got a 500 word email from a student saying why do you always talk about Muslims. It wasn't a nice experience. (Interview 9)

This demonstrates the way in which racially marked academics are more prone to receiving 'constant and unwarranted criticism of their teaching' (Lazos 2012b: 466). Such criticism and backlash are entrenched within a broader politics of racism which serves as a tool to discipline their agency within the classroom setting. The next respondent goes onto elaborate this point:

> We know BME people will always consistently get worse student feedback. On the one hand you might think that's because white men are just better teachers, but when you look beyond the surface you know that's not the case. Many students are just often very uncomfortable with the presence of BME lecturers. Most of my feedback has been positive but I've had some negative, very directed comments, and one thing I always remember is a student writing that my teaching is always very one sided, and that I'm biased, or that I failed to talk about white 'victims' of racism. (Interview 13)

Lazos argues that due to the fact that students may not have the tools to deal with their resentment, (both conscious and unconscious), 'they may discharge their feelings' in complaints or giving poor feedback (2012b: 466). Furthermore in many cases, as also supported by my interviews, students often hold perceptions that their lecturers are 'ideologically driven,' a point frequently made explicit in student feedback (ibid.: 181; Chan et al. 2014: 15). Student evaluations therefore pose a number of challenges and implications for racially marked academics who are perhaps evaluated less on their performance and more on their racialized and gendered subjectivity—and what is (negatively) attached to them.

In addition to this, the widespread implementation of lecture capture (a tool that records lectures for students to have at their disposal), concerned many of my respondents. While the arguments for lecture capture claim that it is an important pedagogical tool that enhances student learning, particularly helping those with disabilities, the negative consequences for racially marked academics cannot be underestimated. As we have seen, racially marked lecturers are more likely to receive criticism from their students due their ingrained racial (and gendered) biases. Against an already hostile backdrop of white resentment the added pressure of lectures being recorded potentially poses some major difficulties for racially marked academics:

> I often feel like I'm under surveillance with the students, so there are times where I do push the envelope, but there are times when I know I have to be so careful about how I respond and what I say. I dread lecture capture, because my freedom in the moment to just respond and engage and provoke is more and more limited. Why? Because my provocation could be interpreted by white colleagues and students as something else – and that's terrifying. So this style of teaching is increasingly shut down, it's not seen as a gift. And if it turns out badly, so someone is offended, or feels unduly put upon for whatever reason, then there's a record. (Interview 20)

Although the purpose of lecture capture is purportedly not to assess or evaluate teacher performance we can see that it could easily be used in such an insidious way. With the levels of surveillance of racially marked academics that already takes place within universities, lecture capture could certainly serve as another mechanism to monitor them. Lecture capture is particularly dangerous for racially marked academics as we are so often the ones teaching sensitive topics, and as we have seen, *we* have to deal with the negative consequences and backlash of that labour. Because such issues are politicized in nature and over-determined by our racial and gendered identities, we are more vulnerable to further evaluation and scrutiny by students and staff through lecture capture, whereby our comments could—as is most often the case—be misunderstood and misinterpreted. The respondent rightly points to the way in which lecture capture has the possibility to close down academic freedom and undermine our agency within the classroom. Lecture capture as a surveillance tool will only subvert the pedagogic relationship between lecturers and students in the university setting, as it imposes a greater set of restrictions and limitations on teaching practice.

Student Cohort: Differences in Russell Groups and Post-92s

The type of institution can sometimes make a real difference to experiences of teaching. My participants worked in both Russell Group universities and Post-92 universities. Without generalizing Post-92 universities tend to have (but not always) a more diverse cohort of students from different racial and class backgrounds compared to Russell Group universities, which remain stubbornly white and elite. For the most part Post-92s fare better in terms of diversity, but demographics often vary from context to context. Nonetheless, there was a sense that racially marked academics did experience key differences in the types of institutions that they taught within, and commented on the positive impact that it had upon them when teaching a larger cohort of students from BME backgrounds, for example:

> When I first started teaching in a Russell Group, I really felt a sense of posh whiteness from the students I was teaching, and they were so self-confident, and I'd be like how are my students more confident than me? It was really weird. My teaching has varied so much across the

institutions in which I've taught. While my first experience was with a bunch of very privileged students, luckily other institutions haven't been nearly as bad. And that's made such a difference. (Interview 16)

She goes onto say:

> In Russell Groups your ability to teach is brought into question and you can see that students are evaluating you all the time, so I think I experienced a much greater sense of anxiety there. But then when I moved to another teaching post, half my students were of BME backgrounds and I loved it so much. I was so happy. The teaching experience was great, students were making connections with me and that was really nice, I've never had that before. It was clearly important that they were being taught by someone that looked like them. (Interview 16)

The notion of 'posh whiteness,' privilege, and overconfidence from the students that the respondent taught at a Russell Group university are not all too surprising, as such institutions are commonly regarded as the 'preserve of the privately educated White upper-middle class' (Boliver 2013: 347). Russell Group universities can therefore be seen to actively reproduce and maintain a politics of elite whiteness. This is perhaps most clearly evidenced by extensive data that consistently shows that those from Black and Minority Ethnic backgrounds remain strikingly under-represented in Russell Group institutions, and are less likely to receive offers from these universities (Boliver 2016: 261). Research by Vikki Boliver for example found that, 'whereas nearly a quarter of all the university entrants classified as White entered Russell Group universities, this was the case for just 6 per cent of Black Caribbean/African entrants and only 12 and 18 per cent of Pakistani/Bangladeshi and Indian entrants respectively' (2013: 351). Interestingly, when the respondent moved to a non-Russell Group institution her teaching experiences were far more positive, as she was in an environment with greater racial and ethnic diversity, this clearly made a difference to both her and her students. This was picked up by another respondent who said:

> One of the nicest things about my teaching is that where I work (Post-92) I have a large cohort of South Asian students and I can tell I have a

positive impact on them. They'll come to my office because they feel like they can come to me for support- which says something bad about the rest of the department, but it's nice to know I can make some kind of difference. (Interview 12)

Again we are presented with a positive teaching experience whereby both the educator and the students are involved in rich, supportive exchanges. The following participant further commented upon this:

As someone who is South Asian from a working class background with the accent that I have, I think it's unusual for students to see someone like myself as a teacher, standing up at the front of a lecture hall at a Russell Group university, saying the things that I'm saying. It's exceptional, and once or twice I've been abruptly interrupted in this context. My relationship with my students has however, been largely positive, particularly at Post-92 universities, because of the connection that they feel, whether real or perceived, because of how I look and how I sound. (Interview 14)

The next respondent also stated that:

It's interesting because BME students all come to me and look up to me, they feel safe in some respects. My university education didn't actually equip me to understand the racial world that I was in, I didn't have the tools to understand or analyse it – I wasn't given them tools. And that's one of the things that I'm trying to rectify with my students, the BME students love it. (Interview 9)

From the various responses it appears crucial for students of colour to both see and experience racially marked academics within their universities. Such presence allows trust and confidence to be built which are fundamental for BME students if they are to thrive and survive white, hostile environments (Housee 2008: 247). Both Russell Group and Post-92 universities perhaps need to recognize the value of having both a diverse student body and a diverse teaching faculty if they are to effectively counter the inequality, marginalization, and alienation rife within their institutions.

Emotional Labour

For racially marked academics the psychological strains of teaching in British universities cannot be underestimated (Sian 2017: 15). Chan, Dhamoon, and Moy put forward a convincing argument that this form of emotional-intensive labour should be regarded as 'institutional contractual or collective agreement issues,' rather than individual problems (2014: 20). This is perhaps more urgent a task in light of extensive research that continues to expose the realities around 'race-related life stress' experienced by racially marked subjects (Franklin et al. 2006: 14). We mapped this out in the previous chapter in relation to departmental politics, but this chapter has also shown that issues around stress continue to follow racially marked academics within teaching spaces.

Harlow argues that the amount of time and energy involved in 'impression management' that is, trying to convince their students of their abilities and legitimacy, can take an emotional and physical toll on racially marked academics (2003: 359). In addition to this we have also seen the emotional labour attached to teaching race-related subjects which highlights that such a task should not be left only to racially marked academics (Chan et al. 2014: 20). Teaching on such areas is not only likely to generate poor student evaluations, due to students' opposition to having their normative views challenged, but also leads to a sense of dread, isolation and deep feelings of anxiety (Sian 2017: 15), as one respondent commented:

> I've been lecturing now for 8 years and I can't get past these experiences, that experience of whiteness is so stifling. I can't believe I'm still being torn down by these white students – my blood pressure is being raised, I get sweats, and my heart rate goes faster in these situations. (Interview 9)

The respondent demonstrates the actual physical and mental effects of his experiences around teaching in antagonistic environments; he talks of raised blood pressure, sweats, and increased heart rate. This is suggestive of the violence and damage that can often be produced in hostile teaching spaces, whereby the respondent feels constantly 'torn down' by his white students. This has impacted upon his self-confidence and self-esteem, and is a clear indication of how some white students are perpetrators of racial hatred and bullying, which have very real effects for the subjected.

These experiences of racism are emasculating, debilitating, and 'emotionally draining' (Harlow 2003: 362), furthermore they are indicative of a climate of unchecked white resentment. Senior managers need to ensure that 'zero tolerance' policies on racism and discrimination extend to protect members of staff, and that racially marked academics in particular are made aware of the routes that they can pursue if they find themselves in situations where students have subjected them to racist abuse. Racially marked academics should not have to accept or tolerate behaviour that deliberately sets out to make them uncomfortable or anxious in the classroom. We can see the real dangers that racially marked academics can often encounter in unsafe white teaching spaces. The above response was not isolated as the next respondent also spoke of his increased anxiety levels as a consequence of various student provocations:

> I think students try to test me because of my profile, so someone who doesn't fit the typical white middle class male who comes from an Oxbridge background. I think they feel emboldened to challenge me because of my demographic, and I believe that if I had a different profile they wouldn't challenge me in the same way. I feel like they deliberately provoke me. It's been troubling to deal with and I'm still not sure what the perfect way is to deal with that. It makes me anxious. (Interview 13)

The sense of 'emotional vulnerability' that racially marked academics encounter in the classroom setting is clear (Chan et al. 2014: 3). Another participant spoke of the psychological steps that she takes as she enters the classroom:

> Sometimes, I'm walking in class and I hope no ones going to say something, and in the end I don't even want to talk about race anymore because I'm so scared that someone will say something. I'm always scared, so I have to prepare myself psychologically that they might say something. (Interview 2)

She goes onto say:

> I dwell on these things. I haven't had that much experience of lecturing so I'm not comfortable in this position. They think I don't deserve to be there. I don't have anyone who is around me who isn't white so it's difficult to talk to people at the institution. So when dealing with all the stuff against me from the students, I don't really have many mechanisms. (Interview 2)

We see clearly in the response that in the absence of institutional support, racially marked academics are often compelled to reflect upon, and question, if they are 'fit' for this kind of labour (Niemann 2012: 450). We have also seen that there is a clear lack of support from the wider white faculty, who fail to engage with not only teaching sensitive issues, but also in supporting racially marked academics encountering hostile teaching environments. The feeling of limited support from white colleagues was further commented upon by the following respondent, who recalled an incident whereby a white professor was in disbelief that racism or conflict could arise in the classroom:

> We did a workshop on training around teaching and difficult situations that could arise between staff and students. For me I'm constantly thinking that something like this could happen, as I'm a woman and 'Asian looking'. Now the white male professor chairing this session seemed very surprised to hear that. He was like, 'oh has anyone had an experience of a conflict in the seminar setting?' I think I've always expected that to happen at any moment in my teaching career, and it surprised me that the white male professor was sitting there shocked saying it had never happened to him in his life. I don't think many white male professors realize how privileged they are. The fact that they don't realize how much privilege they have suggests to me that they don't understand how challenging it may be for other people, including myself. (Interview 7)

The responses indicate both a lack of awareness and a lack of interest from white members of staff around the complex ways in which systemic racial violence may operate in the classroom, and the extensive emotional labour that is involved in managing these situations

(Sian 2017: 18). Institutional racism is thus so entrenched that practices of racism become increasingly obscured by white privilege (Franklin et al. 2006: 14). The reluctance of whites to reflect upon the way in which racial (and gendered) power dynamics operate within teaching environments suggests that they are perhaps apprehensive about challenging structures that they directly (and indirectly) benefit from (Sian 2017: 18). The silence, the lack of support, and the trivialization of racism by white members of staff, works to reinforce racialized and gendered structures which continue to privilege them. If the university seeks to promote rich, critical learning, and positive pedagogical exchanges, senior managers need to do far more to address the needs and challenges experienced by racially marked academics in the classroom.

Conclusion

This chapter has discussed the main issues confronting racially marked academics in teaching spaces, as Lazos reminds us, 'minority professors must negotiate many more burdens than non-minority professors from the first moment that they walk into the classroom' (2012a: 183). From whitelash, to negative perceptions and questionable evaluation processes, racially marked academics are faced with real threats and dangers from white students in the classroom. Teaching environments are perhaps unsurprisingly unsafe spaces for racially marked academics, as they are situated within a wider institution that actively reproduces systematic forms of racism. We have seen the sobering realities for racially marked academics who are undermined, disrespected, and continuously challenged and scrutinized, by a white majority student body. There is clearly a gendered element in the responses that racially marked academics receive from their students, while males are subjected to direct forms of abuse, females are often treated as bodies that lack authority and credibility.

The data has shown that there are clear power dynamics and tensions operating in teacher–student relations, which racially marked academics are continuously required to negotiate. It seems clear that for the most part students of colour strike a positive connection with racially marked academics, unfortunately however, because their presence is so limited these connections can only be few and far between. Despite the backlash that racially marked academics face in the classroom my participants have shown an incredible sense of resilience and strength, as they actively reflect upon their pedagogical practice. Such reflexivity is to be praised and demonstrates that they will not allow their experiences to tear or wear them down; rather they have shown their capacity to bounce back and continue in the face of challenging and hostile environments.

As previously mentioned, I cannot overstate enough times the need for both senior and non-senior members of staff to support racially marked academics, particularly those at early career stages, who are perhaps more vulnerable to, and less prepared in dealing with, racial antagonism. As racially marked academics the emotional labour and personal investment that goes into teaching cannot be underestimated. Universities therefore have a responsibility to make systemic changes that seriously consider the various factors that negatively impact upon racially marked academics in the classroom (Lazos 2012a: 185), that is, structural shifts need to take place to ensure that racially marked academics are protected and supported at all times.

Notes

1. See, for example, Clara Wilkins (2017) whose study found that whites who do not welcome social progress, respond by defining themselves as victims of racism/discrimination, *The Conversation*, 19 December 2017: http://theconversation.com/the-dangerous-belief-that-white-people-are-under-attack-88622.
2. For further details, see: 'Students "Don't Trust Lecturers Who Aren't Native Speakers",' *Times Higher Education*, 15 November 2017: https://www.timeshighereducation.com/news/students-dont-trust-lecturerswho-arent-native-speakers.
3. The Teaching Excellence (TEF) refers to a national exercise that was introduced by the government in England. It evaluates excellence in teaching and universities and colleges across the country are required to partake to measure how well they ensure excellent outcomes for their

students. The National Student Survey (NSS) collects opinions and feedback from students about their universities and the courses on which they studied. The data gathered provides public information about higher education and universities across the country.

References

Bailey, A. (2017). Race and the Naming of Whiteness. In G. Yancy (Ed.), *On Race: 34 Conversations in a Time of Crisis*. New York: Oxford University Press.

Boliver, V. (2013). How Fair Is Access to More Prestigious UK Universities? *The British Journal of Sociology, 64*(2), 345–364.

Boliver, V. (2016). Exploring Ethnic Inequalities in Admission to Russell Group Universities. *Sociology, 50*(2), 247–266.

Chan, A., Dhamoon, R., & Moy, L. (2014). Metaphoric Representations of Women of Colour in the Academy: Teaching Race, Disrupting Power. *Borderlands, 13*(2), 1–26.

Essed, P. (2000). Dilemmas in Leadership: Women of Colour in the Academy. *Ethnic and Racial Studies, 23*(5), 888–904.

Franklin, A. J., Boyd-Franklin, N., & Kelly, S. (2006). Racism and Invisibility. *Journal of Emotional Abuse, 6*(2–3), 9–30.

Harlow, R. (2003). "Race Doesn't Matter, but…": The Effect of Race on Professors' Experiences and Emotion Management in the Undergraduate College Classroom. *Social Psychology Quarterly, 66*(4), 348–363.

Hendrix, K. G. (1998). Student Perceptions of the Influence of Race on Professor Credibility. *Journal of Black Studies, 28*(6), 738–763.

Housee, S. (2008). Should Ethnicity Matter When Teaching About "Race" and Racism in the Classroom? *Race Ethnicity and Education, 11*(4), 415–428.

Lazos, S. (2012a). Are Student Teaching Evaluations Holding Back Women and Minorities? The Perils of "Doing" Gender and Race in the Classroom. In G. Muhs, Y. Niemann, C. Gonzalez, & A. Harris (Eds.), *Presumed Incompetent: The Intersections of Race and Class for Women in Academia* (pp. 164–185). Boulder: University Press of Colorado.

Lazos, S. (2012b). Lessons from the Experiences of Women of Colour Working in Academia. In G. Muhs, Y. Niemann, C. Gonzalez, & A. Harris (Eds.), *Presumed Incompetent: The Intersections of Race and Class for Women in Academia* (pp. 466–467). Boulder: University Press of Colorado.

Matias, C. (2018). Tell the Devil I'm Back: A Self-Reflection on the Radical Possibilities for Racial Justice. *Taboo: The Journal of Culture and Education, 17*(1), 5–14.

Matthews, D. (2017, November 15). Students "Don't Trust Lecturers Who Aren't Native Speakers". *Times Higher Education*. https://www.timeshigher-education.com/news/students-dont-trust-lecturers-who-arent-native-speakers.

Ng, R. (1993). A Woman Out of Control: Deconstructing Sexism and Racism in the University. *Canadian Journal of Education, 18*(3), 189–205.

Niemann, Y. (2012). Lessons from the Experiences of Women of Color Working in Academia. In G. Muhs, Y. Niemann, C. Gonzalez, & A. Harris (Eds.), *Presumed Incompetent: The Intersections of Race and Class for Women in Academia* (pp. 446–501). Boulder: University Press of Colorado.

Purwar, N. (2004). Fish In and Out of Water: A Theoretical Framework for Race and the Space of Academia. In I. Law, D. Phillips, & L. Turney (Eds.), *Institutional Racism in Higher Education* (pp. 49–58). Staffordshire: Trentham Books.

Reid, L. (2010). The Role of Perceived Race and Gender in the Evaluation of College Teaching on RateMyProfessors.com. *Journal of Diversity in Higher Education, 3*(3), 137–152.

Runnymede Trust. (2010). *Ethnicity and Participation in Higher Education* (Policy Briefing Paper). London, 1–4. https://www.runnymedetrust.org/uploads/Parliamentary%20briefings/HigherEducationNovember2010.pdf.

Sian, K. (2017). Being Black in a White World: Understanding Racism in British Universities. *International Journal on Collective Identity Research, 176*(2), 1–26.

Vo, L. (2012). Politics of Elusive Belonging. In G. Muhs, Y. Niemann, C. Gonzalez, & A. Harris (Eds.), *Presumed Incompetent: The Intersections of Race and Class for Women in Academia* (pp. 93–112). Boulder: University Press of Colorado.

Wilkins, C. (2017, December 19). The Dangerous Belief That White People Are Under Attack. *The Conversation*. http://theconversation.com/the-dangerous-belief-that-white-people-are-under-attack-88622.

5

Decolonizing the Curriculum

Introduction

Interrupting hegemonic forms of knowledge in British universities requires a deep sense of structural transformation. From my own experience of years of being based within sociology departments, it is with confidence that I can say that the social sciences have been central in reproducing Eurocentric knowledge formations. This knowledge is based on a narrow and reductive set of ideas to maintain an ontological distinction between the 'modern' and 'civilized' West, and the 'primitive' 'uncivilized' Non-West (Hall 1992: 275–331; Patel 2014: 606). Calls to critically challenge the institutionalization of these knowledges are not to suggest that universities should simply eradicate European ideas, but rather to recognize the limitations of these concepts within pedagogical practice across disciplines (Patel 2014: 609). The introduction of the first Black Studies programme at Birmingham City University,[1] and the *Why Is My Curriculum White?* campaign,[2] both demonstrate successful mobilizations around the possibility of unsettling conventional university curricula (Peters 2015: 643). Such projects illustrate the significance of carving out epistemological spaces for educators and students

© The Author(s) 2019
K. P. Sian, *Navigating Institutional Racism in British Universities*,
Mapping Global Racisms, https://doi.org/10.1007/978-3-030-14284-1_5

to engage with 'other' knowledges, and situate global issues in nuanced, critical frameworks. Decolonizing the curriculum is thus vital to ensure both the transformation of higher education and the development of outward looking spaces.

Much of the literature on decolonization has emerged notably in the outposts of the Global South in the Global North. These analyses developed as a way to think through colonial histories of violence and have pioneered the critique of colonial ways of thinking (and doing). This body of work actively engages with what Boaventura de Sousa Santos (2014) describes as the 'epistemologies of the Global South' that is, understandings of the world that go beyond Western frameworks by examining alternative ways of thinking, as well as valuing the diversity of knowledge; in other words, disrupting the hegemony of Eurocentrism (Santos 2014: 70). Debates around decolonizing education aim to challenge the (re)production of colonial knowledge, as Juliana McLaughlin and Susan Whatman suggest, decolonizing knowledge in higher education both requires and involves, 'a deep sense of recognition of and challenge to colonial forms of knowledge, pedagogical strategies and research methodologies' (2011: 366). Calls to decolonize the curriculum seek to introduce different histories, alternative philosophies, and broader concepts, which combine to displace, or rather, decentre, Eurocentric thought and practice within the academy.

Decolonizing the Curriculum

It could be argued that Edward Said's *Orientalism* is perhaps one of the key texts to have lay down the foundations for building an intellectual project around decolonizing the curriculum. In his critique of Orientalism, he offers us a rich, critical account into the ways in which European or Western thought remains systematically privileged in narrations of the 'other' (1978: 201). These accounts become hegemonic in organizing common sense understandings of the ('superior') West and the ('inferior') Non-West. Said carefully details the processes by which these discourses have become institutionalized in universities, governments, and the arts, to name but a few (ibid.: 202). As he argues,

'The Orient that appears in Orientalism, then, is a system of representations framed by a whole set of forces that brought the Orient into Western learning, Western consciousness, and later, Western empire' (ibid.: 202–203). Orientalism is thus a political project that denies non-Western cultures voice and agency. The Orientalist enterprise has undeniably been embedded, and continues to be reproduced, in educational systems throughout the West. If we take school textbooks for example, it comes as no surprise that those from 'other' cultures are read through a reductive, Western lens, as they continue to reaffirm the logics of Orientalism. A key example is a case which hit the headlines in 2018, whereby it was reported that a GCSE Sociology textbook was rife with essentializing, racist stereotypes about Caribbean families, it read:

> In Caribbean families, the fathers and husbands are largely absent and women assume the most responsibility in childrearing. When men and women live together, it is usually in cohabiting or common law relationships that reproduce the traditional patriarchal division of labour. (Badshah, 8 October 2018: *The Guardian*)

If we take Said's analysis seriously, it should come as no surprise that statements of this nature continue to inform mainstream British curriculums in primary, secondary, and higher education. In my own experiences as a student, I frequently stumbled upon literature around South Asians bursting with descriptions of 'culture clashes,' 'oppressive households,' 'traditional customs' and 'passive women' (Sian 2013). What these examples point to is the dominance of Western knowledge production. In his later work *Culture and Imperialism*, Said revisits some of these debates and argues that:

> …The schooling for such relatively provincial thought and action is still prevalent, unchecked, uncritically accepted, recurringly replicated in the education of generation after generation. (1994: 21)

Said is perhaps calling for us to check, to be critical, and to develop counter-narratives, as a way to resist and interrupt the centrality of Western discourses; this is the heart of decolonizing the curriculum.

He goes onto outline some practicalities of what this might actually entail, proposing that, 'we must expand the horizons against which questions of the *how* and *what* to read are both posed and answered' (ibid.: 385). He urges us to recognize that texts are linked to politics, that they 'require attention and criticism,' (ibid.) and that, 'reading and writing texts are never neutral activities' (ibid.). He argues that, 'we cannot deal with the literature of the peripheries without also attending to the literature of the metropolitan centres' (ibid.), in other words Said is calling for a global analysis, not one that simply excludes particular knowledge formations, but rather that which critically attends to a wider body of work, which is both cognisant and reflective of the power dynamics shaping the production of particular ideas, thoughts, and practices.

Said's account leads us nicely into the work of Walter Mignolo, who has been central in critiquing the European narrative of 'modernity,' which he argues masks its darker side, 'coloniality' (Mignolo 2011). I have previously explored some of these themes in my earlier book, *Conversations in Postcolonial Thought* (2014). A key argument I presented was that the while the core objective of sociology (and the social sciences more generally) is to examine the development of modern society, it paradoxically fails to consider colonial systems and racist practices which were central to the establishment of modernity (Sian 2014), as Mignolo puts it, coloniality in such contexts serves as, 'the secret shame of the family, kept in the attic, out of the view of friends and family' (2011: xxi). University curriculums across Britain have been instrumental in the concealing of European colonial histories and legacies. For Clelia O. Rodriguez, 'we must scrutinise the logic of power that is behind our syllabi and our research work. If we are truly committed to decolonizing we must listen to the silences' (2018: 33). Attempts to decolonize the curriculum are thus motivated by the objective to ensure that universities seriously engage with, reflect upon, and address the implications of these practices both conceptually and practically. The continued neglect and opposition to do so poses major consequences for students and staff in a fast changing global and political climate.

This critique has gained momentum over the past few years, and has, as we have already seen, been a key intellectual argument for many decades. In the public domain however, the debate is perhaps not all as new as we may think it is. I was first introduced to attempts to decolonize the curriculum back in the early 1990s through the popular American TV sitcom, The Fresh Prince of Bel-Air.[3] This points to how mainstream the debates around decolonizing curriculum had become in the US as early as the 1990s, and how my engagement with these issues was vicarious. It also signals to the marginality of these topics in popular British culture, and demonstrates the power of the American television industry to act as a vector for the global dissemination of ideas surrounding the whiteness of the curriculum. The episode of particular interest entitled, *The Ethnic Tip*, first aired in 1991 and is based around Will's attempt to get Black history taught in his American history class. After being called up on his poor marks, he complains to his Aunt Viv that, 'We don't learn nothing about the Black people in American history.'[4] Sympathetic to his frustrations Aunt Viv says, 'Don't just complain, baby, take action! Write a statement about why more Black history should be added to the curriculum. Present it at next week's parent-teachers' meeting.'[5] Will follows her advice and outlines his argument at the meeting:

> We learn about George Washington and Thomas Jefferson and them other dudes that wound up on money but what about Martin Luther King and Crispus Attucks and all the other Black people that made a difference in this country?[6]

To which the teacher responds:

> First, in my course, we are trying to condense 200 and some odd years of history into nine months of lessons. Obviously, we have to concentrate on some historical figures and exclude others. Second, our school has a fine library, or so I've been told where any student can study more about Black history. Third: For years I have taught my course from this well-respected textbook and quite frankly, I don't know a lick more than what's in this book. So forget it... It certainly will take some time to revise the curriculum[7]

Not to simply reduce the decolonizing the curriculum campaign to an episode of Fresh Prince, but the exchange nonetheless is interesting as demonstrates the various tensions between those calling for change, and the all too familiar response with which that call is met. As we will see in the reflections below, that same sense of strain is experienced by those that I interviewed, who faced similar institutional challenges. My respondents all saw the value of decolonizing the curriculum, however spoke of the various barriers that they faced concerning senior management, the nature of the disciplines, and wider institutional structures, for example:

> I have been an observer of the decolonizing the curriculum movement in my department and have been a supporter of the idea. In my own module I am trying to mitigate the overwhelming preponderance of European writers on my reading list. We tend to frame and structure things poorly across our programmes, which marginalize works and ideas from non-Europe. In my experience the first time students encounter people of colour is in their second year, and that is for only one week. Students generally are not taught well about Empire and colonialism. (Interview 17)

The next participant speaks directly to the difficulties he has faced around curriculum reform:

> I think to make the curriculum more reflective of the world where we are right now, in my experience is met by two different objections. On the one hand, I've had colleagues say that we can have more classes on saris, steel bands and samosas, but mainly at undergraduate level. Other times they say we shouldn't bring identity politics into the curriculum; it's not about black or white, it's about teaching what's right. In my experience the university makes up its mind and rationalises its decision; so positive feedback and robust recruitment all go by the wayside once their mind has been made to stick to a particular policy which downplays race and decoloniality. (Interview 5)

Another respondent raised key concerns around the fact that British universities and their curriculums fail to promote the change necessary to ensure that students can speak to the current global political climate, she said:

Universities need to have or find the sensitivity to make the institution relevant and responsive to the social world we live in. They keep promoting the same old shit, but that's just not relevant anymore to our current world and lives. In the disciplines yes keep the classics, but bring in themes and arguments that are contemporary and relevant to the global world we live in now. But then there is a sense that it's not going to shift, until the ranks fill up with people that look like you and I. Because if you think about it, the curriculum didn't shift towards gender until there were women in the place. So in the upper echelon of the university, the VCs, the senior academics, the board members and the Senates, those places need to be coloured and gendered in ways that they're not now. (Interview 20)

The responses demonstrate the way in which intellectual agendas in British universities operate to maintain a narrow, inward looking perspective that reinforces Orientalism and whiteness/Europeaness; such a vision is sustained and reproduced by those at the top. As a consequence, the current curriculum can only work to relay particular forms of knowledge which are deeply rooted within ideas around Western superiority. This was reflected by the next participant who said:

The status quo in my field is that the clock began from the Ancient Greco civilizations and the ideas and the concepts have been borrowed from that particular tradition. And what that ignores is the violence that's been necessary for those ideas to emerge and appear as natural. The curriculum doesn't reflect the genealogy of most disciplines and the power dynamics that exist or have existed in producing them. The curriculum in this sense is racist because it silences voices in histories in particular moments. This is rarely questioned by students- the disciplines are presumed to be natural. (Interview 14)

He went onto comment that:

In all my years of teaching across different universities there has never been any attempt to recognize the plurality and the multiplicity of the traditions in the disciplines, or their entanglements with history and politics. Institutionally these debates are seen as marginal or irrelevant. I think moves to diverse reading lists for example are certainly welcomed, but remain very much the exception rather than the rule. (Interview 14)

It was clear from my responses that there was a lack of institutional support and resources to implement meaningful change at the structural level. It was almost always left to the individual to diversify teaching materials, or such work came from student led initiatives. The responses reflect the continued disinterest by senior management to invest within this issue:

> My department is not invested in this kind of work, the only activity I've seen in my university on decolonizing the curriculum has been PhD led, so its not something that's embedded in the structure. The curriculum is too white, too male and out of date, and there's no desire at the top to change that. (Interview 13)

This was echoed by another participant who said:

> For me the head of the department should say this whole week will be dedicated to studying non-white theory and we will put it on the curriculum, and we will take what is relevant and we will add it to our teaching. If there's not someone higher up forcing them to do it, then they're not going to do it because they don't have to. (Interview 2)

The following respondent raised a common complaint among my interviewees around the fact that it was left to him to make the necessary changes required to introduce broader issues and thought onto his teaching programmes that had been previously neglected:

> The teaching when I took it over, none of it had race in any of the literature; if it was present it was all just kind of textbook definitions with no criticality. So for that reason I felt obliged to change some of that curriculum for my own teaching, and adopt a more critical framework in dealing with these issues, in order to help students understand how these things operate. On the reading list when I took on this course, it was all white authors and thinkers. (Interview 4)

Added to this, another respondent while acknowledging the positive changes that had been made in his institution around decolonizing the curriculum, he was also very aware that this was not a collective endeavour, that is, he made it clear that white members of staff were reluctant to engage within such activity:

> There have been moves here around decolonizing the curriculum. We've been able to introduce more writers and thinkers of colour within the content and we've also taken part in surveys to address what we're doing and not doing. It's impressive in a way because we've looked at the teaching as a whole and we have made changes. But this activity has had no impact on white staff members; they're definitely opposed to decolonizing the curriculum, in my experience they haven't welcomed this change at all. (Interview 10)

There was also a sense that for the few institutions that have gradually acknowledged the importance of decolonizing the curriculum, such recognition was less about structural reform and more about market driven logics, for example:

> My department seems to have suddenly realised that there is a market for anti-racist and decolonial scholarship. So it's become a 'niche' area of focus as a way to differentiate themselves. This is a market based approach, so it's only based on the idea that more students will come to take prospective courses, rather than being about social justice. As soon as the market forces change, the university will move away from that and focus on something more marketable. So as long as it's dependent on the market, I don't think race has the longevity or the structural approach that we need. (Interview 12)

Another participant commented that:

> Decolonizing the curriculum should have been addressed years ago. At my university we're looking at our reading lists. I think these developments are really good; it's long over due. It's good to see it on the agenda, but that's only come about because universities have recognised that its an issue they need to support otherwise they'll get left behind. (Interview 11)

My respondents pointed to the significance of decolonizing the curriculum in terms of offering students a wider, global, and critical perspective. They also spoke of the dangers arising if universities continue to fail to provide students with broader, diverse knowledge, as one participant said:

> I think universities need to think carefully about what they represent. If the university is about generating new knowledge for particular subject areas, they need to reflect on existing knowledge and think about integrating new forms of knowledge from other parts of the world. I think there still remains a strong sense of British superiority in academia and the curriculum perpetuates that position which is very problematic. (Interview 15)

Similarly another respondent commented:

> If nothing else to teach in sociology is to give critical tools to see the social world and the power imbalance, and I think that's very important. So by not having non-Western theorists or readings it's almost like we're suggesting the whole western world is the leader in knowledge. (Interview 7)

Sujata Patel argues that in order for the social sciences to be more global in character, they must, 'deliberate the many different experiences of modernity' and 'critically reframe the terms of classical sociology' (2014: 604). Patel suggests that three key features may be considered for effective campaigns around decolonizing the social sciences. First, is the commitment to deconstructing 'the provincialism' of Eurocentric knowledge and situating it within its own cultural and national history (ibid.: 609). Practically, this involves changing the syllabus and the curriculum, alongside developing research objectives and methodologies that are reflexive and self-conscious. Secondly, social scientists need to be involved in critically analysing the 'form' of their concepts, ideas, and narratives (ibid.). Finally, social science departments must actively engage in dialogue with activists, grassroots organizations, and communities, to allow for rich insight, reflection, and collaboration (ibid.: 610). Related to this point, Patel calls for the development of long lasting intellectual networks with the Global South (ibid.). Similarly for

Santos the social science curriculum requires profound change, not only to address social problems in the contemporary global context, but also, to reflect the diversity/globality of sociological thinking (2014: 78). For Santos this requires not only the recognition of 'other' voices, but also the recognition of Europe's colonial past and present.

The main problem with the reproduction of Eurocentric knowledge is that for the most part all thinking, practices, and cultures considered to be outside Europe, are more than often conceptualized as inferior. In contrast, European knowledge is frequently heralded as being superior. As such, the institutionalization of Eurocentrism particularly in universities sees, 'the overrepresentation of the White, bourgeois, male, who rationalizes his dominion over those he deems to be irrational, affectable, and inferior' (Andreotti et al. 2015: 24). Social science curriculums (among many others) have therefore been either intentionally, or unintentionally, complicit in the reproduction of reductive Eurocentric/Orientalist epistemologies. Such concerns were raised by my respondents who not only felt that current knowledge production in universities reflected an exercise in coloniality, but also that through the silencing of wider modes of thought students were likely to suffer:

> Our syllabuses, our reading lists, our methods and what is recognised as having educational value is a continued reproduction of imperialism, such that they devalue other knowledge. I have found that the students have only had a narrow learning on a range of issues, and what they find exciting is opening up their minds on those other areas and factors that they haven't typically been introduced to. I make sure that my outlook when teaching is global. This work should be mainstreamed, not just side-lined as it is now. (Interview 19)

Another participant similarly spoke of the dangers arising from current curriculum design and teaching content in British universities:

> The design of the British curriculum doesn't seem to facilitate critical thinking. We have to present the whole picture to students, and this needs to be done much earlier on. Otherwise you get students walking around thinking that these people are heroes because we've selected one piece, but

not the other. We have a responsibility in our teaching to not reproduce racism and it's not up to one individual to do it, it has to be across the whole curriculum. Now white colleagues often say they just want to teach what is valuable to that session, but they don't realise that what's valuable is the political position of the theorist or thinker. We have to be evaluative and critical of the work we use. How dare we skew history to celebrate particular European thinkers, when there are so many other successful, beautiful, interesting, and diverse cultures. (Interview 20)

Echoing the significance of 'other' knowledges, Njoki Wane et al. point out that, 'we are all at a disadvantage when we devalue non-Western systems of thought…Our exclusive entrenchment in one system of thought impoverishes us all' (2004: 509). Perhaps the most commonly articulated opposition to decolonizing the curriculum is the (false) claim that the campaign seeks to make all forms of European knowledge redundant. This silly complaint appears to be more reflective of the insecurities of those in dominant positions, who are not quite ready to let go of their arrogant fantasies of superiority. Calls to decolonize the curriculum do not simply suggest that because the social sciences are European they are 'wrong,' or that we should eradicate European categories and frameworks, as Patel argues, 'we need not reinvent the wheel; however there is a necessity to generate explanations that are relevant for different contexts' (2014: 609). The arguments around decolonizing education as a whole are therefore rooted in the recognition of the limitations of dominant concepts, practices, and tools, within pedagogical spaces. Such reflexivity ensures that students are equipped with more complex and critical understandings of global debates and issues, in other words, the key goal of decolonizing the curriculum is to generate a more productive and insightful account, 'of not only how the world we live in came to be but also how it can be' (Sian 2014: 194). Decolonizing the curriculum is thus vital to both the transformation of higher education, and the development of inclusive spaces.

Vanessa de Oliveira Andreotti et al. argue that higher education has played a significant role in reproducing the violences of modernity (2015: 30–31). However, they also point out that in more recent times, there have been a series of interventions across Western universities, which have seen various forms of resistance by academics, activists, and students (i.e. 'why is my curriculum white?'). Such debates have often grappled with whether or not decolonizing the curriculum is even possible (ibid.). In their study, Andreotti et al. develop a social cartography of responses to modernity's violence, which represents the varied, and often interconnected, commitments (and non-commitments) to decolonization in higher education, see Table 5.1.

As the table demonstrates, in spaces that adopt the 'everything is awesome' approach, decolonization is made redundant. Here the fantasy that there are no problems or issues around racial inequality have been deeply embedded within the institution (ibid.: 32). This goes hand in hand with the idea of the post-racial, which was mapped out in Chapter 2. For Paul Warmington post-racial enunciations in higher education 'remain premature' (2009: 283), and the myth of the colour-blind university environment operates to deny the significance of racism. That is, in this framework (which is currently hegemonic in British universities), critical engagement and reflection with racial and colonial histories are dismissed and viewed with scepticism. Here (white) senior management claim that everyone has equal opportunities, therefore pedagogical decolonizing practices are regarded unnecessary.

When higher education adopts a 'soft-reform' approach, the critique of modernity's violence is likely to be framed in terms of, 'greater inclusion based on the liberal understanding of inequality' (Andreotti et al. 2015: 32). In a similar vein to 'everything is awesome,' in the 'soft-reform' framework, decolonization practices are not required, as inclusion (i.e. giving extra resources to low-income students of colour) is seen to be sufficient enough (ibid.). This approach assumes that excluded groups wish to be part of the dominant culture of the institution, and that they will benefit from inclusion in this way (ibid.). Within this setting:

> The knowledge, skills, and experiences that they bring to the institution are rarely valued, except perhaps through tokenistic 'recognitions' of cultural diversity that make the institution appear to be welcoming, but otherwise do not threaten the status-quo of their operations. (ibid.)

Table 5.1 Different articulations of decolonization in Higher Education, Andreotti et al. 2015: 31

Space	Meaning of decolonization	Practice
Everything is awesome	No recognition of decolonization as a desirable project	No decolonizing practices required
Soft-reform	No recognition of decolonization as a desirable project, but increased access/conditional inclusion into mainstream	Providing additional resources to Indigenous, racialized, low-income, and first-generation students, so as to equip them with the knowledge, skills, and cultural capital to excel according to existing institutional standards
Radical-reform (recognition of epistemological dominance)	Recognition, representation, redistribution, voice, reconciliation	Centre and empower marginalized groups, and redistribute and reappropriate material resources
Beyond-reform (recognition of ontological and metaphysical enclosures)	Dismantling of modernity's systematic violences (capitalism, colonialism, racism, heteropatriarchy, nation-state formation)	Subversive educational use of spaces and resources, hacking, hospicing

The focus here is upon increased access, rather than a profound institutional change that engages with critical reflection (ibid.). This approach contrasts with the 'radical-reform' position, which places greater emphasis on the decolonization of higher education. 'Radical-reform' aims to: increase the representation of minority groups; invest in widening access to higher education for marginalized voices; and reflect critically upon colonial histories (ibid.: 33). Here non-curricular campus activities are also framed as playing a central role in decolonizing the university, examples include: promoting divestment campaigns in support of the Palestinian cause; demanding that universities reflect upon and compensate for their involvement in transatlantic slavery and the genocide of Indigenous peoples; and acknowledging the land of Indigenous peoples' upon which the university has been built (ibid.: 33). According to Andreotti et al. over the past 40 years these efforts have played a major role in the transformation of higher education; successful outcomes have led to desegregation, the formation of Indigenous-controlled schools, and the embedding of excluded knowledges (i.e. African American studies, Indigenous studies, and Ethnic, Queer, and Women's Studies) (ibid.). However, it has also been suggested that despite such shifts, 'the academy maintains a tokenistic and selective commitment to these fields' (ibid.). Furthermore, Andreotti et al. argue that, so long as decolonial practices operate within the existing university system, they are unable to escape the fact that, 'the core business of the university as a credentializing institution for "emancipated" socially mobile subjects will remain intact' (ibid.: 34). In short, this means that 'radical-reform' in practice is unable to successfully promote non-exploitative futures in an increasingly exploitative neoliberal environment.

This brings us to Andreotti et al's. last approach: 'beyond-reform.' In this space, universities are viewed as 'beyond repair' (ibid.). This concern is also addressed by Michael Peters (2015) who questions whether such a space has, 'the intellectual resources within to transform itself and come to terms with the historical effects and traces of racism that are invested in our institutions and in our knowledge traditions' (2015: 645). However, for Andreotti et al. universities can still be useful if 'navigated strategically,' in other words, hacked (Andreotti et al. 2015: 34). The 'hacking' of higher education refers to, 'disenchantment with modernity and the usual perks and rewards that the system itself offers, in favour of diverting its resources towards other ends' (ibid.). Here the focus is upon strategically working within the space to disrupt, and potentially transform, power structures and knowledges.

Decolonial Summer Schools

In his critique of coloniality and modernity, Aníbal Quijano argues the following:

> The liberation of intercultural relations from the prison of coloniality also implies the freedom of all peoples to choose, individually or collectively, such relations: a freedom to choose between various cultural orientations, and, above all, the freedom to produce, criticize, change, and exchange culture and society. This liberation is, part of the process of social liberation from all power organized as inequality, discrimination, exploitation, and as domination. (2007: 178)

In attempts to liberate both communities and students from colonial knowledge productions, the role of decolonial summer schools cannot be underestimated. They offer a real, practical alternative to traditional university programmes and provide important sites for resistance. Since its inception in 2015, I have been fortunate to participate as a core member of the teaching faculty for an annual summer school, 'Racism, Eurocentrism and Political Struggles,' held at the Centro de Estudos Sociais/Centre for Social Studies (CES), University of Coimbra, Portugal.[8] I can honestly say that this has been one of the most rewarding and enriching experiences of my teaching career. The fact that the school operates outside the UK makes a real difference, and although students pay to study here it runs on a not-for-profit basis. There is no requirement for lecture capture, no insatiable demands, and no expectation of an employability package at the end. It is immune from the dark neoliberal forces that have come to subsume British universities, in other words, it most definitely does not operate as a corporation based on a soulless set of mechanical, administrative, capitalist transactions that most of us are all too familiar with in the UK. The purpose of the summer school is to critically address global debates and contemporary struggles against racism and Eurocentrism at three main levels: (1) Knowledge production (2) Public policy and (3) Grassroots and activist movements.

The key goals and objectives of the programme are to reflect upon and critique Eurocentric knowledge formations and understand how these are linked to broader histories of racism, enslavement, genocide and colonialism. The programme seeks to question and disrupt hegemonic concepts and frameworks in political and academic spheres. It examines the implications of key concepts for understanding broader political debates around state racism, violence, nation and citizenship. It is committed to representing interdisciplinary research across international contexts, and promotes a critical analysis of public policies for challenging discrimination. It seriously engages with critical dialogue and alternative forms of resistance proposed by grassroots movements and activist organizations, by reflecting upon the power relations and political struggles that shape these complex exchanges and dynamics.

The school itself is comprised of a range of students from different international contexts. Researchers, educators, activists and postgraduate students attend the school with the view to encounter alternative knowledge and acquire critical tools to deepen their understandings of the world. The faculty is made up of international academics and representatives from activist movements, including the Parti Indigene Republique/Party of the Indigenous of the Republic (PIR).[9] In my experience the students are always engaged, enthusiastic, and actively form connections with one another as a way to work through the issues collectively. The contrast with Britain is really quite remarkable. It is a school that encourages collaboration, rather than individual gain; criticality as opposed to neutrality, and empowerment over profit. Sessions are based around decolonial politics, anti-racism, cultures of scholarship and the politics of memorialization, racism and education, Islamophobia, state violence and activist approaches. The school also hosts arts-based performances.

This for me is symbolic of what decolonized learning and teaching might look like in practice. The discussions are passionate, the space is safe, and the breadth of knowledge engaged with (beyond Europe) is striking. At least four different languages are spoken at the school and presentations are translated for all the students. The environment is supportive, intellectually stimulating and vibrant. The school although still in its infancy continues to grow, and modelled itself on other critical summer schools including: 'Critical Muslim Studies: Decolonial Struggles and Liberation Theologies' (Granada) and 'The Summer School on Black Europe' (Amsterdam). These schools offer important spaces to both disrupt and challenge conventional knowledge formations and productions. Through their engagement with global thought and critical debate, they illustrate the real significance and potential of a decolonized curriculum, and more broadly, a decolonized university.

Conclusion

As thought and practice continues to develop around decolonizing the curriculum we have seen the power and the strength of this movement as a key driver to unsettle conventional curriculums across British universities. On the other hand, we have also seen the various challenges that racially marked academics face in their attempts to implement such change. They remain tightly constrained by university structures that are not yet fully committed to investing in this transformation, despite the positive outcome it sets to bring to all students. As bell hooks warns us, in the absence of profound reform, education will continue to reflect the plantation culture, where the slave was only able to learn forms of knowledge that legitimized enslavement and racial hierarchies (2003: 93). With or without wider institutional support, calls to decolonize the curriculum remain necessary. Beyond investment from the university, political willingness to campaign on the issue is also crucial to systematically embed this much-needed transformation. Under a current hostile Tory government such support is unlikely, however hopes of a Corbyn led Labour government could indeed prompt the action required.

Most notably Corbyn has vocally supported moves to change the current school curriculum calling for the history of the British Empire, colonialism and slavery being taught nationwide.[10] In October 2018, he announced proposals to improve the national curriculum, arguing that it was necessary that schoolchildren learned about and understood the significant role that black Britons had played in shaping both the nation's history and the struggle for racial equality (Crerar, *The Guardian*: 11 October 2018)[11]. He also highlighted the importance of representation, suggesting that the stories and experiences of black British role models—who fought for justice and equality in Britain, as well as those who struggled for liberation from British colonial rule—needed to be told in the classroom (ibid.). He stated that:

> Black history is British history, and it should not be confined to a single month each year. It is vital that future generations understand the role that Black Britons have played in our country's history and the struggle for racial equality. (ibid.)

Corbyn also laid out impressive plans to develop a new 'Emancipation Educational Trust' to ensure that these issues continue to be taught to future generations through school programmes, visits to important historical sites, and engagement with the history of the Non-West prior to colonization (ibid.). Such proposals represent a significant shift in education and demonstrate the exciting beginnings of what a nationwide decolonial curriculum may look like in Britain. While we eagerly await the victory of Corbyn we must continue our own campaigns in our universities, which at the very least continue to alert wider teaching staff about their own limitations forcing them to reflect critically upon their pedagogical practice. As my teaching experience in a decolonial summer school has demonstrated, the commitment to decolonizing the curriculum offers real scope for transformative learning opportunities. Achille Joseph Mbembe perhaps sums this up best when he says:

> To decolonize the university is to therefore to reform it with the aim of creating a less provincial and more open critical cosmopolitan pluriversalism – a task that involves the radical refounding of our ways of thinking and a transcendence of our disciplinary divisions. (2016: 37)

This chapter has demonstrated that serious engagement and critical reflection with campaigns to decolonize the curriculum promises the potential to institutionalize alternative, inclusive futures in university spaces and beyond.

Notes

1. The first undergraduate degree in Black Studies was implemented in 2016 at Birmingham City University. Led by Professor Kehinde Andrews, the programme teaches students about the history, politics, and culture of people from the African Diaspora, and introduces them to different perspectives and conceptual frameworks.
2. The Why is my Curriculum White? movement was founded by students at University College London in 2015. It came as a response to the embeddedness of Eurocentrism and whiteness operating in university curriculums across the UK. The objectives of the campaign aim to both challenge and highlight the lack of diversity within higher education teaching and learning practice.
3. The Fresh Prince of Bel-Air is a hit American sitcom that aired from 1990–1996. The show is based around black teenager, Will, who moves from West Philadelphia to live with his wealthy aunt, uncle and cousins in their Bel-Air mansion.
4. *The Fresh Prince of Bel-Air*. 14 January 1991. NBC. Season 1, Episode 17. Television.
5. *The Fresh Prince of Bel-Air*. 14 January 1991. NBC. Season 1, Episode 17. Television.
6. *The Fresh Prince of Bel-Air*. 14 January 1991. NBC. Season 1, Episode 17. Television.
7. *The Fresh Prince of Bel-Air*. 14 January 1991. NBC. Season 1, Episode 17. Television.
8. For further details see: https://ces.uc.pt/en/ces.
9. Parti Indigene Republique/Party of the Indigenous of the Republic is a decolonial political organization in France led by anti-racist activists. Houria Bouteldja is the spokesperson and a founding member of the party.
10. Jeremy Corbyn is the current leader of the Labour Party, elected in 2015.
11. See: 'Jeremy Corbyn vows to increase teaching of black history in schools,' (11 October 2018): https://www.theguardian.com/world/2018/oct/11/jeremy-corbyn-labour-vows-to-increase-teaching-of-black-history-in-schools.

References

Badshah, N. (2018, October 8). GCSE Textbook Condemned for Racist Caribbean Stereotypes. *The Guardian.* https://www.theguardian.com/world/2018/oct/08/gcse-textbook-condemned-for-racist-caribbean-stereotypes?CMP=share_btn_tw.

Crerar, P. (2018, October 11). Jeremy Corbyn Vows to Increase Teaching of Black History in Schools. *The Guardian.* https://www.theguardian.com/world/2018/oct/11/jeremy-corbyn-labour-vows-to-increase-teaching-of-black-history-in-schools.

de Oliveira Andreotti, V., Stein, S., Ahenakew, C., & Hunt, D. (2015). Mapping Interpretations of Decolonization in the Context of Higher Education. *Decolonization: Indigeneity, Education & Society, 4*(1), 21–40.

Hall, S. (1992). The West and the Rest: Discourse and Power. In S. Hall & B. Gieben (Eds.), *Formations of Modernity* (pp. 275–332). Cambridge: Polity Press.

hooks, b. (1989). Choosing the Margin as a Space of Racial Openness. *The Journal of Cinema and Media, 36*, 15–23.

Mbembe, A. (2016). Decolonizing the University: New Directions. *Arts and Humanities in Higher Education, 15*(1), 29–45.

McLaughlin, J., & Whatman, S. (2011). The Potential of Critical Race Theory in Decolonizing University Curricula. *Asia Pacific Journal of Education, 31*(4), 365–377.

Mignolo, W. (2011). *The Darker Side of Western Modernity: Global Futures, Decolonial Options.* Durham: Duke University Press.

Patel, S. (2014). Afterword: Doing Global Sociology: Issues, Problems and Challenges. *Current Sociology, 62*(4), 603–613.

Peters, M. (2015). Why Is My Curriculum White? *Educational Philosophy and Theory, 47*(7), 641–646.

Quijano, A. (2007). Coloniality and Modernity/Rationality. *Cultural Studies, 21*(2–3), 168–178.

Rodriguez, C. (2018). *Decolonizing Academia: Poverty, Oppression, and Pain.* Halifax: Fernwood Publishing.

Said, E. (1978). *Orientalism.* London: Penguin Books.

Said, E. (1994). *Culture and Imperialism.* London: Vintage.

Santos, B. (2014). Boaventura de Sousa Santos. In K. Sian (Eds.), *Conversations in Postcolonial Thought* (pp. 63–80). London: Palgrave.

Sian, K. (2013). *Unsettling Sikh and Muslim Conflict: Mistaken Identities, Forced Conversions, and Postcolonial Formations.* Lanham: Lexington Books.

Sian, K. (2014). *Conversations in Postcolonial Thought.* London: Palgrave.

The Fresh Prince of Bel-Air. (1991, 14 January). *NBC.* Season 1, Episode 17. Television. USA.

Wane, N., Shahjahan, R. A., & Wagner, A. (2004). Walking the Talk: Decolonizing the Politics of Equity of Knowledge and Charting the Course for an Inclusive Curriculum in Higher Education. *Canadian Journal of Development Studies, 25*(3), 499–510.

Warmington, P. (2009). Taking Race Out of Scare Quotes: Race-Conscious Social Analysis in an Ostensibly Post-racial World. *Race Ethnicity and Education, 12*(3), 281–296.

6

Hiring Practices and Career Development

Introduction

Research continues to demonstrate persistent patterns of racial inequality across British universities. As mapped out in the introduction, data has shown that 92.4% of professors are white, while only 0.49% are black (Garner, 3 February 2015: *Independent*).[1] Figures go onto report that a mere 15 black academics are in senior management roles (ibid.). For racially marked female academics the data paints a further dismal picture, with only 17 black female professors appointed across the country (ibid.). Racially marked academics are on the whole less likely to be shortlisted, appointed, or promoted in comparison to their white counterparts (Pilkington 2013: 229). In addition to this it has been reported that BME academics at top universities across Britain earn on average 26% less than their white colleagues (Croxford, BBC: 7 December 2018).[2] In light of these shocking figures senior managers can no longer deny, mask, or hide the prevalence of racism in British universities. It is a widespread, systemic problem that needs to be addressed with urgency.

© The Author(s) 2019
K. P. Sian, *Navigating Institutional Racism in British Universities*,
Mapping Global Racisms, https://doi.org/10.1007/978-3-030-14284-1_6

On the surface universities have strutted various strategies that seem to promote positive action around gender equality and racial equality. Beneath these jamborees however the reality is dire (for people of colour that is). In 2006 The Equality Challenge Unit was established to support and advance equality and diversity in higher education for staff and students (Equality Challenge Unit 2018). It provides a central resource of advice and guidance for those in higher education, and has developed two charters in order to improve gender equality and race equality across the sector. These include the Athena SWAN Charter and the Race Equality Charter (REC) which both claim to address the under-representation of women and minority ethnic staff (ibid.). The Athena SWAN Charter was established in 2005 to recognize and support the commitment to advancing women's careers in the sector and address gender equality issues (ibid.). Building upon the Athena SWAN Charter, the Equality Challenge Unit developed the REC in 2012. This specifically aims to address racial inequality and improve the representation, progression, and success of minority ethnic staff and students within higher education (ibid.). Universities via their departments are expected to apply for these awards by documenting how they are addressing these issues and the changes they intend to implement. If successful in their extensive tick box submissions they are awarded a shiny badge at Gold, Silver, or Bronze level, which can be plastered on institutional webpages, marketing literature, and job adverts as a way to verify that they have successfully 'done' gender and race equality.

Alongside these national initiatives, universities must comply with the Equality Act (2010) and the Public Sector Equality Duty.[3] Universities also often have their own wider equality and diversity strategy outlining their principles and values, sometimes hiring departmental 'Equality and Diversity Champions' (a tokenistic, and somewhat ironic role usually given to racially marked academics). Despite these seemingly extensive provisions in place, why then is it the case that in 2018 less than 7% of all academic staff in universities across the country came from BME backgrounds?[4] As will be made clear throughout this chapter, such glossy initiatives and policies geared towards race equality are actually motionless in practice, that is, beneath the equality and diversity 'talk' there is no desire for change. The alleged commitments are insincere, unsystematic, and for the most part inactive, that is, their main function appears to be that of a branding exercise rather than a commitment to structural change.

Interestingly however, this is less so the case for gender equality. It could be argued that the advances made by white women in higher education—while by no means complete—certainly shows progress across the sector. For racially marked academics there is still a long way to go in relation to the demographic weight they have in the population. Much of the equalities policy in higher education has enabled gender advancement to the extent by which some disciplines are over-represented by white senior female academics. This appears to demonstrate an imbalance of power suggesting that while white women's career advancement remains a priority, the same cannot be said for racially marked academics where progression in the sector is virtually non-existent, that is, academics from BME backgrounds remain profoundly under-represented at the top. This discussion will be picked up further in the last part of the chapter, first we will identify the processes by which institutional racism operates to create barriers for racially marked academics in terms of career advancement. Most notably this is facilitated by dismal mentoring systems and systematic discouragement around promotions. Perhaps this should come as no surprise since the book has already documented quite clearly that the very foundations of British universities are racist.

Racism, as we have seen, is at the heart of the contemporary British university; it is woven deeply into its structures, its culture, its physical make-up and its day-to-day practices. All these elements combine to keep racially marked academics at the bottom; they are devalued, dismissed, and appear to have only bleak future prospects ahead of them. As I already stated in the introduction to this book, racism is the dirty secret that universities want to hide, and they have successfully done so for decades. These entrenched discriminatory practices are so normalized that they are no longer exceptional. The myth of the post-racial, liberal university is central in maintaining the subordination of racially marked academics in these spaces, as they are led to believe that the university is meritocratic, fair, and equal. This couldn't be farther from the truth, and it will take more than a rubber stamp from the Equality Challenge Unit to change the situation for racially marked academics working within this toxic environment that breeds white privilege, discrimination, and systemic racism.

Lack of Mentoring

Racially marked academics remain unsupported in universities across the country. Research has shown that racially marked female academics are particularly, 'sorely lacking' in access to career guidance from a mentor, often being forced to look in other places for the kinds of support conventionally provided by senior faculty members in their departments (Thomas and Hollenshead 2001: 173; Sian 2017: 20). Robbie Shilliam argues that alongside over-scrutiny by senior colleagues, black academics frequently express a lack of mentorship starting from as early as PhD study (2015: 32). Added to this is the problem of ingrained racial/gender prejudices which work to reproduce, 'white male networks and career advancement' (ibid.). As a result, racially marked academics are disregarded for promotions or discouraged from the application process (ibid.; Sian 2017: 20). For Chan, Dhamoon, and Moy, systematic mentoring programmes for racially marked academics, that are both fully resourced, and driven by non-white members of staff, must be implemented in order to facilitate strong support networks (2014: 20; Sian 2017: 20–21). My respondents expressed that the lack of support in their universities served as a key barrier to promotion and career development, for example:

> I don't think I've been supported at all. When I first arrived I went through an experience where I needed a mentor, but all my support came from outside the school and faculty. I don't get any encouragement for promotion- this university doesn't encourage me at all. I don't get the support networks, I don't get the mentoring, but I get overburdened with teaching. I don't see a future where I will progress. I see my white colleagues being encouraged, but that never seems to happen to me. There really is no support; it's dismal. (Interview 11)

The idea that white members of staff received more support through mentoring was picked up across all of my interviews, as one respondent said:

> The senior people in the department are older white men and women, and they tend to socialize with people who are like them, and they are mentoring people who are like them both officially and informally. (Interview 16)

Another participant went onto comment that:

> When I went to my first academic job, the first thing I did was ask for a mentor, and they put me with this white woman. She was fine, she was lovely, she helped me in the everyday bits of how the university worked, but she didn't help me on a personal level or in relation to things around career progression. I noticed that fairly new white colleagues had got promotions after two years, for very little work, no publications, no university level work, nothing like that - they just got it. They always seemed to be more supported. (Interview 9)

Similar to the experiences documented above, Bhopal's research found that racially marked academics consistently felt that they were missing out on the same level of mentoring that their white colleagues appeared to be receiving (2016: 77). This had the consequence of making them feel excluded, and unable to develop networks and contacts required for both promotion and career advancement (ibid.). The next respondent speaks about the lack of guidance and the lack of interest from her mentor, who didn't appear to be invested in developing any form of relationship:

> I had a faculty mentor assigned to me and I don't even think that person knew that that's what they were for me, which was not very convenient. I'm relatively independent in how I do things, but I do sometimes need assistance with making strategic choices, like publishing. (Interview 17)

Another participant commented:

When I was working at my former institution on a fixed term, one year contract, somebody who I used to really look up to and respect was a white professor there. I constantly searched for support and mentoring in this person but I never got it. He was not supportive, and didn't even engage in conversation with me. (Interview 4)

There was a very strong sense that my respondents had to seek support from beyond the institution (often another country), as the internal networks of support were so limited, as one interviewee noted:

I didn't get any form of mentoring or support. There's nothing internal to the institution, I had to seek out feedback and support myself. My mentoring has come from out of the institution, and sometimes from out of the country, from people who I knew back in the day. But for white colleagues you see there is a solid network there, and it's like a perpetuating machine; they all co-sign each others applications, share each others teaching content, and support one another - and you're are definitely not part of that. (Interview 20)

This was raised by another respondent who said:

My support has been appropriate, but not outstanding. There are many times when I've felt who do I turn to about this particular issue? And I end up going to someone who is on another continent, because in my own department I don't know who to go to for assistance. I remember asking someone quite senior in the department a while back, if I should publish a book, or concentrate on articles, and they just seemed puzzled, like 'why are you asking this? Why would you even ask that?' and I felt stupid for asking. Mentorship has been okay but generally not all that good. (Interview 17)

The next participant similarly speaks of relying on external forms of support, unable to find any source of help and guidance internally:

I've never really known where to go for support or mentoring, particularly in the earlier stages of my career. I think over time it's become a bit easier because I haven't just relied on people within my department or university, I've had to find that elsewhere. You just get used to it, which isn't such a good thing because you stop being so outraged as you realise that's just how it is. So it is isolating. (Interview 16)

There were also concerns around the mentoring processes that were in place being very informal, lax, and generally sloppy overall, with different rules and protocols operating for different people, for example:

I've never had a mentor in a formal capacity, until much later on. I think I may have been told that I had a mentor at previous institutions but we never met, and they mentored someone else unofficially – a white man unofficially became their mentee. (Interview 20)

As the next respondent describes even when robust mentoring appears to be in place from the outset, in reality it is rarely, if at all, practised in such a way:

When I started my job I was told I would have 2 mentors, one a pastoral mentor and the other a more academic, intellectual mentor. That's not really happened because people are so overworked, and it's not really in their workloads. It's not a formalized relationship but we've not built up the informal relationship to make it sustainable. I think a lot of mentoring is often informal, but I've not got that, and it's not introduced formally either. A lot of the support that I've had is from peers at the same level, which does not get me all the mentorship that I need. I don't know what I need to succeed in academia. It would be nice to be in a place where we as academics of colour don't have to ask or feel awkward about asking. (Interview 12)

This experience was further elaborated upon by another participant who complained that no formal mentoring arrangements had been put in place at his institution, and as a result any mentoring that did occur was that which took place with other racially marked academics, rather than somebody assigned to that particular obligation:

I think if there's any mentoring for members of staff of colour, it really is mentoring between ourselves- it's very informal. At no point has anyone sat down with me and said, 'do you think it would be good to have a mentor?' But when it's white colleagues, I often see that someone gets puts in place to mentor and support them. (Interview 10)

Several of my respondents spoke about the importance of being assigned with a mentor of colour, they felt that this might make a real difference to them in terms of support, and also being able to discuss particular issues that a white mentor may not fully understand or necessarily be sympathetic towards:

> I can't be that frank with my current mentor about issues of race and how it makes me feel, because he's not had the same experience. I feel like if I had somebody who was at the same rank as me, from the same background, I would be able to relate better and I think they'd understand my experiences better. I feel that what is missing in my mentor relationship is that sense of being relatable. I go to my outside networks to get that support, and we share those experiences and challenges. I keep a lot of it to myself though, I talk about it with my wife, but then that impinges on my home life. (Interview 13)

Again we see that the respondent has had to resort to external networks for support. Christine Stanely points out that a 'one size fits all' mentoring model is problematic for racially marked academics who are unlikely to develop a strong relationship with a colleague that fails to understand their particularities and lived experiences (2006: 713–714). The problem of course is that there may not be enough racially marked academics in the department for this approach to work, as we have seen clearly so often is the case that there are only at best a handful of racially marked academics in departments across universities in Britain, and at worst one, and they tend to be in junior positions, therefore mentoring of this kind will be limited unless of course hiring practices transform. If racially marked academics are lucky enough to find an official—or more likely—an unofficial mentor of colour, they are perhaps more inclined to discuss difficult issues and receive the advice and support that they need from those who have already been through similar challenges, and who have often experienced racism in the academy first hand:

> I think I have had a lot of support, but I'll stress that it doesn't seem to have been from people in power or influence, which is significant. I'm very grateful that people have given me time and advice. A colleague of colour

who was very good to me actually hardened me to not expect anything. So any liberal delusion that one might hold, he more or less disabused me of that. So he taught me that nothing's going to go in my favour- so there was a degree of harshness. I guess it's a little like, not to draw misplaced analogies, in America they talk about the talk with black families to their black children about police – and that's quite a disheartening talk to disabuse a child of any innocence. In some ways I think many of us have had that kind of talk with our respective mentors. (Interview 18)

It is rather sad that these talks still have to happen, and as the respondent points out, they are indeed taking place on a frequent basis. I know in my own experience that over the years my mentor of colour has had similar conversations with me. The participant is right to suggest that we do become hardened as a result, and learn not to expect anything from our institutions. As hinted at throughout the book, without the support from my mentor—in helping me to develop a thick skin, preparing me for knock backs, and constantly making the time to listen and guide me through issues both big and small—I can honestly say that I don't think that I'd have found the strength to stick it out. In such an isolating, racist space, I cannot stress enough the importance of mentorship from a person of colour. They provide a safe space for you to laugh, cry, prepare, and plan—it must of course be emphasized that this labour is invisible, and unpaid; they do it off their own bat, particularly if they are external. They do it because they actually care about your progress and advancement, they do it because they want you to succeed, and they do it out of selflessness and solidarity. My mentor has been a blessing; through constant support I have grown, developed, thrived and picked myself up time and time again. My mentor helped me to be strong, resilient, and fearless, and for that I will always remain indebted. I am very aware of the rarity of such an occurrence; for the most part the reality for many racially marked academics is that they are simply left to figure things out on their own:

I don't think there are enough institutional mechanisms to support academics of colour. I didn't get much mentoring about careers post-PhD and I thought that was completely normal. I wasn't given any indication as to how important publications were, future research proposals, books and so on- that's the stuff I had to learn largely on my own and I learnt that quite late on. I thought this was normal and it wasn't until I had the job I have now that I realised it's not normal at all- you are meant to get support and tutelage. I almost felt guilty getting support from my current boss because it was so unexpected, and he assured me that it was his job to do that. (Interview 14)

He goes onto say:

> I think universities need to recognise the value of mentoring, and also recognise the structural issues nascent academics of colour face. I wouldn't want my mentor to be just another white person, they'd have to be someone who could recognise the issues and challenges we have to endure and help us navigate them. I wouldn't want simply liberal recognition. (Interview 14)

Undeniably mentoring and support for racially marked academics, from those who understand particular issues and struggles, remain vital and have the potential to make a real difference both on a personal and professional level. Evidently this is not happening at all to the extent that it should be, which poses many consequences for racially marked academics in terms of career advancement and general wellbeing, as noted in the responses below:

> For promotion the issue of mentoring is crucial, and a lot of that is informal and relies on who you know. For people of colour that is one major obstacle. (Interview 5)

And:

> We need more mentoring, I know I've struggled so much as a result of that lack of mentoring. I feel like I'm constantly fighting. (Interview 9)

This section has shown that racially marked academics are at a real loss without proper mentoring. So often is the case that we go to other racially marked academics (externally and informally), who take on mentoring in an unofficial capacity. This support has often been crucial for us, and as the next chapter will demonstrate, it represents an important site of resistance. Through these informal networks we are able to guide, help, and support each other collectively through the challenges that we all encounter in the white academy. However, at the same time it is utterly disgraceful that we have had to actively seek support in other places as a result of our own institutions failing to provide us with sufficient or appropriate mentoring. The fact that such a basic form of support is not guaranteed to us by our line managers is shameful, especially when we see our white colleagues appearing to receive formal mentoring and training. It is crucial that all members of staff receive equal levels of support and guidance that is actually helpful, and that which facilitates properly our development and advancement within the sector.

Exceptional Just to Be Ordinary: Promotion and the Politics of White Cultural Capital

When I think of Pierre Bourdieu, I am reminded of an extract in Laurent Binet's, *The Seventh Function of Language,* and I can't help but laugh:

> The American asks: 'What about Pierre Bourdieu – isn't he a good philosopher… The publisher explains to the American that Bourdieu is a sociologist who did a lot of work on invisible inequalities, and cultural, social, symbolic capital… Sollers makes a show of yawning. 'Above all, he is boring beyond belief. (2018: 126)

I must confess, I have never really understood the fascination with Bourdieu who seems to remain a staple of British sociology curriculums. However, at risk of digression I want to bring in his thesis on cultural capital in particular. For brevity Bourdieu's cultural capital refers to the ways in which the cultivation of knowledge, manners, poise, style, behaviour, interests, and skills can indicate one's cultural proficiency, which in turn establishes one's social standing in society. I have no qualms with this analysis—drummed into me when I first embarked upon sociology—however, I think it is also very important to recognize that Bourdieu is speaking specifically to whiteness. In the field of education there has been much debate around the extent to which cultural capital can simply be equated to whiteness. For example, in his critique of cultural capital as that which is synonymous with whiteness, Derron Wallace argues that such a conflation is reductive as it takes away the nuances and complexities of black middle-class identities (2018: 480). While I recognize the importance of taking into account the varied and complex subjectivities produced by race and class, I still maintain that within the traditional Bourdieusian conception of cultural capital, there is a specificity made, or at least implied, to that which signals whiteness.

To elaborate, the various attributes and descriptions deployed to capture cultural capital are those which relate to, and cluster around, specific European, White cultural practices. As such, my understanding of cultural capital as denoting whiteness is not simply a lazy collapsing of the two concepts, but rather it is a recognition that the articulations and iterations of cultural capital—which have been reproduced in the university setting—are those which can only describe a particular privileged experience of whiteness, which will always disprivilege non-whiteness regardless of the actual economic, or social standing of racially marked subjects. At the same time this does not mean that I am simply falling into the trap of reproducing the 'deficit view of communities of color' (Yosso 2005: 82),—i.e. they are at fault—which Tara Yosso is rightly critical of in her deconstruction of cultural capital. That is, I do not argue that racially marked communities signify 'places full of cultural poverty disadvantages' (ibid.), instead the interviews have explicitly demonstrated, and will continue to illuminate, the strengths of the 'other' forms of capital possessed by racially marked subjects, thus in doing so this account aligns itself with Yosso's focus on cultural wealth as a form of empowerment.

Yosso argues that racially marked communities nurture cultural wealth through 6 key forms of capital (ibid.: 77), these include:

1. **Aspirational capital**: The ability to hold onto hopes and dreams for the future, even when encountering actual and perceived barriers/obstacles.
2. **Linguistic capital**: The intellectual and social skills obtained through interactions and communication in more than one language and/or style.
3. **Familial capital**: Those cultural knowledges cultivated by familia (kin) that hold a sense of community history, memory, and cultural intuition.
4. **Social capital**: Networks of people and community resources that provide guidance and emotional support.
5. **Navigational capital**: Skills for maneuvering through various social institutions/contexts.
6. **Resistant capital**: Those knowledges and skills adopted through oppositional performances that challenge inequality/injustice (ibid.: 77–81).

These other forms of capital, as we will go onto see particularly in the next chapter, are those which many of my respondents allude to, or identify, as being important for their progression and resilience within the academy. By listening to the experiences of those at the bottom (ibid.: 82), I have been able to centre the alternative forms of capital that racially marked academics deploy in an environment structured by racism. By doing so, we can demonstrate how racially marked academics are able to use and draw upon their own lived realities as sources of empowerment and advancement, despite the various challenges and barriers that they encounter in the university setting. The struggles, journeys, and narratives therefore point not to victims of racist structures, but rather to agents navigating racist structures. What has been, and will continue to be described throughout this chapter (and more broadly the book), are not simply attempts made by racially marked academics to acquire traditional, white forms of cultural capital, but rather those which actively interrupt whiteness through the recognition and embedding of their own forms of cultural wealth within the academy.

Sociologists for the most part have fallen into the trap of reproducing the notion that people of colour have no (political) class identity, that is, they can only be read and understood through an (apolitical) account of ethnicity—it could indeed be argued that Bourdieu is guilty of reaffirming this assumption. Class has therefore operated as the preserve for whiteness. The failure to recognize varied intersections tends to assume a universality, which remains limiting when accounting for the experiences of people of colour. To that end, I would restate that Bourdieu's cultural capital might be best re-described as white cultural capital—in other words, all the various indicators and traits one has to accumulate in order to be regarded in high esteem is that of which is assigned to the category of whiteness. For example, knowledge refers to European knowledge; behaviour/manners is that of 'civility'; interests and skills is perhaps shorthand for European classical music, European art, European literature, European sports and so on (I'm afraid Kabaddi, fluency in Urdu, the sounds of Public Enemy, and the poetry of Rumi wouldn't quite make the cut here!).

These codes and significations are continually reproduced by the university system. Therefore in order to be held in high regard racially marked academics are expected to learn, adopt, and assimilate into these white values, if they are to succeed. They have to learn and perform whiteness in order to climb the ranks. For racially marked academics, economic capital is rarely ever able to trump white cultural capital. That is, even if racially marked academics come from wealthy backgrounds, they will almost always still be read through a racist framework of 'poor immigrants,' where it is assumed that they hold a deep affection for British education, to the extent that when *we* do get jobs in universities, *they* have done *us* the favour, and *we* should be thankful.

Such assumptions can be seen to fall into the framework of what S. Sayyid describes as the *Immigrant Imaginary*. That is, a pool of highly mobile tropes that have been reproduced to establish an ontological distinction between ex-colonial and ethnically marked settlers (Sayyid 2004: 149–156). Naturally, ethnically marked settlers are situated as unfavourable in comparison to the majority community, in other words they are read through a racist lens that positions them as 'backwards,' 'uncivilized,' and 'primitive' (ibid.). To have any hope of career advancement racially marked academics are therefore left with the difficult/impossible task of learning whiteness, that is, cracking white hidden codes and infiltrating white networks where mysterious opportunities and breaks seem to happen time and time again for white members of staff.

Racially marked academics will, for the most part, follow policy and procedure to a tee, due to the fact that we know our bodies are subjected to scrutiny and surveillance as discussed in Chapter 3. We are also perhaps blissfully unaware, or naively optimistic that the university is indeed meritocratic, and therefore if we follow the rules we will advance due to our extensive profile of achievements. Alas, if only this were the case, for the game—as racially marked academics know all too well—is unequivocally stitched up in favour of whiteness. It comes as no surprise then that many of my respondents, despite having all the skills and knowledge, often found themselves continuously blocked from promotion and career advancement opportunities that were frequently afforded to their less established, white peers. The inability to access (white) hidden rules or (white) hidden networks—i.e. white cultural capital—was a common experience across my interviews whereby respondents felt that their future prospects, particularly in terms of promotion, were negatively impacted as a consequence, as one participant said:

> I've always struggled to know what the rules are, I've gone to sessions on what you need to do to get promoted, but I think there's a whole set of hidden rules that I don't know or that I can't find out and that's frustrating. (Interview 20)

Another respondent commented:

> Encountering white networks has been my experience throughout my career, where I've seen white colleagues get certain opportunities which I have never even known about. You never find out about these opportunities. I often feel little things like perhaps the way I speak or my mannerisms don't fit what they want. (Interview 16)

The next interviewee also recalled these similar exclusionary practices of whiteness:

> I feel my head of department has not only failed to support me, but has also actively blocked me from pursing certain opportunities. He doesn't praise me, I'm not a dog that needs my head patted, but he will support others (whites) over me, definitely. He tends to lobby against me and blocks my opportunities. If I did have his support I could have had so many more doors opened, but because I'm not in his white clique I don't have the same access to those networks. I'm looking for acknowledgement, I'm looking for respect and I'm looking for the same as what other white colleagues get in terms of treatment. I've been treated really poorly compared to others over a consistent amount of time. I feel powerless. (Interview 13)

As can be seen quite clearly, there is a sense that racially marked academics are failed when it comes to career development, whereby they are constantly dismissed and discouraged by their line managers. In addition to this they also have to demonstrate their capabilities and achievements to a far greater degree than their white colleagues:

> I've taken on the work, but I've not got the promotions that go with the stages as I've taken more work on. I know people are less experienced than me, who might have a similar role, but are on higher pay and at a higher grade. I look at the rate at which white colleagues are promoted and I often think how have they got that? I thought promotion was to be based on your value and what you put in, and it seems that isn't the case. This is definitely about race. (Interview 10)

The sense that white colleagues are able to climb the ladder with fewer barriers was a frustration that all my participants shared. My respondents felt that they had to constantly over-achieve in comparison to their white counterparts in order to be considered or acknowledged for promotion, for example:

> I've got publications, I've been conferencing, I've done media work, and I've set up committees at the university level. I'd built a strong reputation in the university and I more than surpassed the requirements for

promotion. I went into a meeting with my Head of School and he said to me, 'its not your turn yet, we'll see what happens next year.' I did actually get the promotion the following year, but I got it along with white colleagues who had half the CV that I had. I learned then you've got to excel to be in a position that a white person can just walk straight into. (Interview 9)

The next respondent picks this up, and speaks about the way in which racially marked academics have to be 'exceptional just to be ordinary':

They can walk into jobs because they have the correct complexion – so they're not competing for the jobs they have. It's like Chris Rock; he has a stand up piece where he says how he lives beside a dentist. He's at the top of his game – one of best comedians in the world – and his neighbour is a white guy who is a dentist. And that's the perfect example of how we have to be exceptional just to be ordinary. And I'm so sad this has manifested in HE the way that it has. There's no reprieve for us, there's no meritocracy. (Interview 20)

The example of Chris Rock given in the above response brilliantly reflects the lengths that racially marked academics (and people colour more broadly) are required to travel in order to be seen on the same level as an average, non-descript white, middle-class individual. When interviewed for the HBO documentary, 'The Black List,' Chris Rock says: 'Who lives next to me? What's the white man next to me? He's a dentist. He didn't invent anything. He's just a dentist. That's what America is' (Ali 2015). This demonstrates clearly the politics of white cultural capital, whereby people of colour are continually expected to be at the top of their game in order to be considered on par with a less established individual that is white. Thus going back to the earlier argument, no amount of achievements or awards can surpass whiteness, in other words, meritocracy in the academy is a myth. The similarity and the frequency of the experiences around this particular dynamic were quite remarkable:

In academia it seems to be a lot more about judgement, so are you good enough to be promoted? Have you done enough? I've been here for more than six years now and I came in at the most junior grade, after having ten years of work experience in other places. I've had over twenty published journal articles, I've got two million pounds worth of funding, and it was only this year that the Head of Department said, 'oh maybe you should put in for promotion'… I feel like in my department they champion certain white people, and I haven't really had any of that. (Interview 3)

Another participant further pointed to both the lack of interest and support that he received when applying for his promotion to Chair:

When I was applying for promotion, my manager took a very laid back approach. So when I informed her I'd like to do this, she said 'well if you want to, I suppose it's okay.' There was not so much encouragement there; she was not supportive at all. The support is not there. It is there for white females, where I've seen colleagues being pushed for promotion when they have less qualifications, experience, and publications than me. (Interview 19)

The next interviewee also spoke of a clear lack of encouragement from her Head of Department for promotion:

I think I should have been promoted by now, on paper I can see that I've met all these criteria, but my Head of Department was not very supportive claiming I'd not done a big enough administrative role, despite the fact that I have actually done lots of substantial admin roles. I think maybe they're right, but I don't feel they are. Then when I look through other people's profiles I quickly see that they've not done this other particular role. And I look through their publications and see that I've got three times as much. It's frustrating. (Interview 20)

The following participant suggested that 'code-switching' and performing whiteness were the only means by which racially marked academics could successfully progress within the sector:

We have to perform cultural whiteness, it gets you far in academia, so adopting a particular vocabulary for example that will get you recognized as 'credible' or having some kind of 'expertise'. These are all associated with the cultural whiteness embedded within the university. We have to do a lot of code-switching. (Interview 17)

Code-switching refers to the practice of performing and communicating in different ways subject to particular social contexts (Waring 2018). In institutions governed by whiteness, people of colour often deploy techniques of code-switching in order to develop and improve their prospects, as Chandra Waring points out, 'the ability to code-switch is often a prerequisite to becoming a successful black person in America' (ibid.). Code-switching can come in different forms including dressing differently or speaking differently (ibid.). Jacques Rangasamy suggests that institutional languages are part of 'race-making' processes (2004: 30). He points out that such a language in the university setting operates to maintain and reinforce a culture of whiteness which excludes and dismisses non-white bodies. This is particularly reflected in the area of career advancement and promotions, as he goes onto describe:

> The language of some institutions generates and supports systems of some cultural behaviour proper to the organization of diversity, but on the terms of the dominant sector, using it's monocultural white, male and middle class notion of fairness to safeguard interest. (ibid.)

Rangasamy further argues that:

> Therefore, communicative competence, which in terms of institutional language consists of a thorough grasp of institutional rules and regulations does not automatically qualify everyone for career progression – as non-white staff in British universities have long realised to their cost. The control over promotion and other rewards of progression is a function of ownership of the institutional language and of the status quo. (ibid.)

Rangasamy's account alerts us to the way in which the institutional language of the university articulates a particular ethos, which is described as, 'a kind of knowingness, an unspoken entente' (ibid.: 31), it is that which, 'encodes the unwritten criteria and caveats that regulate entrance into the inner life of the institution, and access to the privileges of progression, that comes with a genuine sense of belonging' (ibid.). This captures the experiences of exclusion documented by my respondents, and the various ways in which they are continually stifled and suppressed by institutional white codes and practices, that are so routinized and deeply embedded within the university. In addition to navigating these complex performatives of institutional racism, another barrier confronting racially marked academics, particularly in the social sciences, is that concerning the value that is attached to the work and research that they do. For the most part many of us tend to be working on issues around race and ethnicity, or related subject areas: sometimes out of choice, and sometimes out of necessity. However these topics are often met with disdain, disproval, and disparagement from our white colleagues who show a lack of interest or support in our research, unless of course if they can market it as 'doing diversity,' as one respondent commented:

> I think my work is mainly valued in terms of the diversity agenda and community engagement, I think in academic terms it's less valued. I think my research is probably not seen as being central to sociology, other areas are just seen to be more influential in terms of what's required to be a 'renowned' sociologist. (Interview 16)

Again this highlights the way in which the work that racially marked academics undertake fails to fit the white canon of what is deemed 'serious' 'high quality' or 'respectable'—that is, our work is likely to remain in the realms of Rumi, rather than Rousseau:

> A key issue issue is how the work that academics of colour do is valued. There is a racist lens which finds it easy to conclude that if an academic of colour is researching a topic it must be about race, ethnicity, etc. or what they consider to be marginal issues. There is also a racialized expectation that high flyers are always packaged as white. All of these things, I have experienced directly in my prospects for promotion. I was never told what was necessary to get promoted; I was never encouraged to apply. I was discouraged, and my work was seen as being of only marginal interest despite international recognition. I was always left with the suspicion that if I had been white all my accomplishments would have been seen as exemplary and the department would have promoted me. (Interview 5)

The next participant speaks of a similar experience whereby the promotions committee deemed his achievements as unambitious because he had published in non-Western outlets:

During my promotion process, I was being challenged from one particular white professor, which is the reason I didn't get the Chair in the end. He claimed that my work did not make a significant impact on British or American scholarship, because it was based on Africa and not published in Western journals. In the first meeting I had with my mentor, she told me all the journals that I had been publishing in, did not show ambition. My work is multidisciplinary and global, and I deliberately choose the journals that I want to write in. It's a disgrace. (Interview 19)

For Rangasamy, universities have over centuries evolved on entrenched notions that white, straight, wealthy, privileged men are endowed for university culture and their success through the ranks is thus 'natural' (2004: 32). These values, he argues, remain at the core of universities and govern the structure, the management and the decisions of the institution, which are derived from these particular groupings (ibid.). As such, white staff members only celebrate their own culture and their own people, while degrading and dismissing 'others' (ibid.). One respondent went onto point out that she felt that prospects of future promotion could be harmed if one's expertise is located in the field of race:

If you are true to yourself and talk about your work as focused on racism or anti-racism in your CV or cover letter, you run the risk of not being short-listed. (Interview 8)

The sense of feeling unappreciated was common to all my respondents:

There's no real engagement or desire to utilise the skillset that you bring to the table…I found the disconnect to be quite severe when it came down to supporting me as a member of staff. I've done some quite high profile things but there is a reluctance to support me. (Interview 4)

As Rangasamy argues, institutions will often celebrate or champion the achievements of some individuals (white academics), while ignoring and dismissing others (racially marked academics) (2004: 31). He goes onto suggest that creating opportunities for select (white) individuals is another common tactic—which we have seen also revealed in the data—to prevent the progression of particularly those who display a sense of agency (ibid.: 32). Alas, Rangasamy goes onto argue that those racially marked academics brave enough to challenge rejections or unfair decisions are often charged with accusations of 'aggressiveness' 'arrogance' or 'playing the race card,' they are also expected at the same time to be mindful of white fragility and broader white sensibilities (ibid.). It is fair to say that racially marked academics are severely constrained when it comes to the (im)possibility of career advancement in the university setting; this depressing structural reality might help us then understand more critically, why so few racially marked academics occupy senior positions within the sector.

The barriers that racially marked academics encounter when attempting to progress in their careers are really quite daunting. To add insult to injury we are often seen as being 'over-ambitious' if we apply for promotions, and 'over-sensitive' when we are rejected. We are presented with patronizing management spiel claiming that negative outcomes are the result of the 'prematurity' of the applicant, bureaucratic decisions, or failure to meet a criterion (despite clear evidence of the contrary): in other words, white senior management will say anything and everything *but* the real, underlying issue, which boils down to that of racial discrimination. Furthermore, when it comes to the value that is attached to the research that we conduct, we find ourselves constantly being judged according to exclusionary standards of whiteness, which persistently classify our research as 'low quality.' What remains clear is that such a judgement is most certainly not based upon meritocracy, but rather on that of racism, which operates to block, limit and obstruct our chances of progression within the academy. Racially marked academics are required to work more than double in comparison to their white peers, yet for the most part their research and achievements continue to be undervalued and dismissed. These processes combine to prevent racially marked academics from having any hope of breaking through the glass ceiling, however at the same time, because we are aware of the workings of racism we do not simply fall into the trap of self deficit theorizing, but rather we adopt alternative tools to resist and thrive, this will be examined in further detail in the next chapter.

Precarious Contracts and Decision-Making Practices

Discriminatory practices in interview panels/decision-making committees serve to impact negatively upon racially marked academics, both at the level of promotion and recruitment more generally. Decision makers are almost always made up of a few, select, white senior colleagues who bring with them a set of white cultural expectations that immediately shut out racially marked academics. Here certain judgements and decisions will be made including questions of (in)competence, 'careful' considerations around if the candidate 'fits' or is indeed 'worthy' of the opportunity, and the (negative) value that is often attached to the research of the applicant. Racially marked academics frequently experience exclusions based upon these unfair, yet all too familiar, practices. This is not to argue that all decisions made not to hire/promote racially marked academics are racist (Niemann 2012: 492), however at the same time we cannot simply overlook the reality of institutional racism, as demonstrated most clearly by the gross under-representation of racially marked academics in universities, both at junior and senior levels. The struggle for racially marked academics to secure permanent contracts or climb the ladder (as discussed above) would further support this.

My respondents described the various barriers that they felt were in place preventing them from accessing employment opportunities within the sector and raised key concerns around recruitment strategies, interview panels, and decision-making processes:

> We need more BME representation in particular roles to address recruitment practices, like sitting on interview panels for example. People tend to appoint candidates similar to them. So if you have a panel of people who are white and middle class, obviously they will identify with a candidate that is also white and middle class, and who speaks the same kind of language; who is able to perform whiteness. I think different criteria's are used and applied when judging those from BME backgrounds. (Interview 15)

The participant alludes to the way in which recruitment practices often work to perpetuate and reaffirm the university's already existing culture of whiteness, as Ahmed argues, whiteness in this sense becomes the 'ideal' of the organization (2012: 40). The notion that a different set of criteria or that different kinds of judgements were applied to racially marked academics, was elaborated upon by the next respondent who commented:

> On interview panels, if a person appears confident for instance, if it is a white person it is confidence, if it is a person of colour it is seen as arrogance through and through. If you are humorous and white, you are just humorous, if you are a person of colour you are not serious. (Interview 18)

The respondent alludes to the way in which different (negative) signifiers are often attached to non-white academics. Rangasamy argues that regularly it is the case that while universities may comply with procedures around recruitment and progression, they tend to focus on, or point out, the weaknesses of people of colour and 'play down' their strengths, however engage in the opposite when it comes to white candidates (2004: 29). He goes onto suggest that such practices are routine and 'caricature the abilities of both whites and non-whites, and undermine confidence and trust in the system' (ibid.: 30). Therefore, it is not so much the rules and regulations that govern particular decisions, but rather how those in power chose to (re)interpret these rules and regulations in order to to generate/manipulate certain outcomes (ibid.). The next respondent spoke of the hidden practices and agendas operating to prevent racially marked academics from entering or progressing within the system:

> I was encouraged to apply to make my post permanent, but then other people got involved and they pushed their own agenda. So while I had support from an ally, which was really important, other people with different priorities and relationships with people who they wanted to install within those positions, meant that the interview was just a show – they already knew who they wanted – somebody white - but I didn't know that at the time. (Interview 20)

Another participant speaks of a similar experience, whereby despite his strong reputation within his department, he remained on a rolling contract unable to secure a permanent position. He also points to the way in which a white colleague had more support and more strings pulled at the institutional level facilitating a very different outcome:

Whist at my previous institution I had a wider perception of being particularly able, strong on teaching and intellectually interesting, but they still didn't give me a permanent job. So in spite of my reputation no institutional levers were pulled, whilst a good friend of mine, who was white, I know had a few more processes activated into their benefit, so that they could secure an internal line into a job. I think that's very telling, that one can be exceptionalized simultaneously to being expendable. I was there for four years in total on a rolling contract. (Interview 18)

Feelings of being 'expendable' or 'disposable' were common across my interviewees who frequently identified that employment opportunities tended to be rigged in favour of white candidates. Job stability is arguably even more challenging for racially marked, international academics due to work visas and sponsorship (Sian 2017: 21). This adds an extra layer of exclusion, and precarity around securing positions in the academy (ibid.), as one respondent recalls:

As a foreigner I have a lot of issues around my visa, and this process has been really unsettling. Being on a temporary contract and also being part time means that I can't apply for a work visa, because a work visa applies to full time jobs that need to be sponsored by the university. The contract I'm on now is only 50 per cent, and the support has been limited. Having to hold a working visa drastically reduces the chances of me getting employed, because a lot of times, institutions don't have the money to sponsor a visa. The centre I'm based in is very small, there are only a few permanent positions, but all of them on those posts are white. I'm the only non-white staff member there, and the only one on a temporary contract. It's interesting. What's even more devastating is the fact that some of my colleagues will never understand the difficulties or stress I feel which is very problematic. The director didn't even realize in my case that I am a foreigner and if I'm working here I need a visa. That gave me a shock. (Interview 7)

She goes onto state:

I feel like I have less chances of employment compared to white British people. There are challenges around working as an immigrant in the UK, so we may be qualified and may even almost get the position, until the moment we have to tell them that we need a work visa and sponsorship from the university; that's when it falls apart. It feels like we're almost inferior to other people even if we have the qualifications, knowledge and experience. So I often feel less confident about my position. (Interview 7)

Bridget Anderson argues that immigration controls are as much about the conditions of stay as they are about the conditions of entry (2010: 309). That is, non-citizens who have entered the UK legally are likely to encounter particular discriminatory restrictions subject to their visa status (ibid.), and as described in the above case, the respondents' job security is dependent upon a sponsor. This sense of precariousness is further reinforced by the fact that the employer has the power to withdraw sponsorship at any time (Sian 2017: 21–22). Consequently workers subjected to immigration control are placed upon fixed-term contracts that can be ended at the employer's discretion (ibid.), and as expressed by the participant, this has repercussions beyond the workplace contributing to feelings of temporariness, fear, and instability.

The continued denial of opportunities for racially marked academics in higher education can damage their confidence and sense of worth. Furthermore as Rangasamy argues, the practices of denying and devaluing some, while rewarding and supporting others have their roots in European colonial strategies to ensure the continued subordination of colonized peoples (2004: 30). Decisions therefore not to hire or promote racially marked academics, both from 'home' and 'overseas,' are symptomatic of broader colonial logics that serve to safeguard and preserve whiteness.

Athena Swan and the Race Equality Charter: Championing Who?

As mentioned at the start of the chapter British universities have implemented various diversity schemes to apparently ensure representation across disadvantaged groups, namely through the REC and the Athena SWAN Charter. However despite these strategies the persistence of widespread racialized inequalities would seem to suggest that they are having very little, if at all, any impact. In this sense these diversity initiatives might best be understood as being part of a superficial marketing exercise, rather than that of a serious commitment to structural change, as Ahmed suggests:

> The language of diversity certainly appears in official statements (from mission statements to equality policy statements, in brochures, as tag-lines) and as a repertoire of images (collages of smiling faces of different colours), which are easily recognizable as images of diversity. (2012: 52)

She goes onto argue that, 'diversity has a commercial value and can be used as a way not only of marketing the university but of making the university into a marketplace' (ibid.: 53). The increasing focus on diversity (rather than anti-racism) can therefore be linked to the wider manoeuver-ings of senior management to further propagate the myth of the post-ra-cial university. My respondents were unsurprisingly sceptical of new diversity agendas being pushed by their universities. There was a sense that particularly in relation to the representation of people of colour, these strategies were ineffective, however at the same time they pointed to the way in which there seemed to be a greater emphasis and seriousness placed upon white women's representation and advancement, for example:

> I think there are a lot more spaces and networks for tackling gender issues, but these are pretty much all white spaces, and they are exclusion-ary towards people of colour. (Interview 20)

Another respondent commented:

> I think at some point we have to recognize that white women are the majority in many social science fields, and this raises different ideas of orthodoxy and structure. Why is there no such push to advance the pros-pects for academics of colour in the same way as white academic women? (Interview 18)

Similarly:

> There needs to be more awareness and a full implementation of race equality policy. Current policy under the Athena SWAN is targeted only towards white women and that needs to be addressed. (Interview 11)

This does raise the question as to why it appears to be the case that white female academics are more supported in terms of the equality agenda compared to racially marked academics (and in particular, racially marked female academics), who are not even close to matching the level of progress achieved by white women in the university. This was a concern raised by one of my respondents who said:

> I participate in this group which looks at equalities and diversity, and it just seems to focus on the gender stuff, perhaps for various logistical reasons. So other protected categories - like race - are marginal. When you prioritize something you also deprioritize another, and that tends to be the people, particularly academics of colour, who can fight their corner the least. So increasingly we focus on one thing, in this case gender, at the expense of something else like race. (Interview 3)

The side-lining of race has been a persistent practice in the academy; race is overlooked, trivialized and outright ignored in most British universities. As the respondent suggests, race equality is not seen to be a priority in the larger workings of the institution. This unwillingness to engage with race seriously has detrimental effects on racially marked academics and will continue to do so in the future if it remains off the agenda in such a way. The lack of representation of racially marked academics in senior management roles is surely an indication that structural reform around race equality is an urgent and pressing matter. Alas, if only this were the case, as many of my participants suggested any movement towards race equality is mere lip service by senior management:

> There's a naivety around some colleagues, while they are happy to give you lip service about race equality and so on, they're not willing to stake out any processes, because unfortunately, they do have to volunteer sacrificial labour to create the opportunities for academics of colour. (Interview 18)

Another respondent commented:

> Less than 1% of BME people hold any top positions in the academy, it is appalling, in 2018, 21st century Britain – it is appalling. Universities need to move away from lip service on diversity to real practice.

Universities need to stop deselecting academics because they are black or brown or minorities, and they need to recognise that these people will enrich the knowledge and the educational space. BME students have no role models. (Interview 19)

He goes onto state:

Diversity should not be about promoting white, British, middle-class women to high positions as a tokenism of diversity. It should be raw based diversity that should be based on equity, so I for example am not required to do thrice what my colleagues need to do in order to be promoted or to be valued. Universities need to see that our work does not need a white stamp of approval in order to be recognised, we should be recognised because our work has merit. (Interview 19)

Ahmed's work on diversity remains significant here for understanding the processes and practices that keep race equality off the agenda as described by my participants. To have this discussion we must also return to the start of the book and remind ourselves of the post-racial discourse circulating within contemporary British universities, for this phenomenon is deeply intertwined with the disavowal of racism that we see being enacted across higher education. Post-raciality has functioned to trivialize racism and at the same time hide its presence or obscure its reality. Racism is often seen as a 'difficult' issue for managers to deal with, as Ahmed points out, 'racism is not spoken about by those who speak for the university' (2012: 146). Racism and 'race-talk' provokes all kinds of uncomfortable responses in white people, some we have already mapped out throughout this book. Charges of racism, institutional racism, and race inequality disrupt the liberal conception of progression and advancement, as a consequence they are, 'heard as an accusation that threatens the organization's reputation as led by diversity. Racism is heard as potentially injurious to the organization' (ibid.). This constant lack of recognition and failure to acknowledge racial inequality fuels the fabrication that universities are free from racism, and in the process those who point to it are more than often seen as disruptive troublemakers.

Therefore to talk about racism and to draw attention to it is to 'become the problem' (ibid.: 147). Institutional racism and exclusionary practices of whiteness are issues that can rarely, if at all ever, be spoken about, because what is at stake is not a commitment to social justice and racial equality, but rather the reputation of the institution (ibid.). In this way the reluctance by universities and their white managerial cohort to even engage with the language of anti-racism is a strategy adopted to essentially protect whiteness, and in doing so, diversity (rather than anti-racism) represents a key mechanism to safeguard (and reassert) the dominant culture. Diversity is thus used, 'not only to displace attention from material inequalities but also to aestheticize equality, such that only those who have the right kind of body can participate in its appeal' (ibid.: 151). My respondents all recognized that these processes were operating within their institutions, for example:

> All this talk of diversity is a joke. I'm the only person in my department, and there are at most maybe two others in the faculty who are non-white. If you want to find diversity in the university look no further than the cleaning or the catering staff. First thing I see in the morning, if I'm there early, is the black cleaner who will be cleaning and vacuuming and scrubbing the toilets, and that's where diversity is in the university, if you want to find diversity it's there, in the worst jobs, in the most menial and poorly paid jobs which in most cases will be insecure. The higher up you go the whiter it gets. At the very top it's white, and it's impossible to penetrate, where do you even begin? There's no investment there for BME staff and students. (Interview 13)

The respondent demonstrates how 'diversity talk' in the university cannot be taken seriously, particularly when the everyday, embodied and structural context explicitly shows that institutional racism is rife. This was picked up further by another one of my interviewees who remained critical of diversity initiatives around racism:

> Is it going to change? I know a few universities are going for the new Race Equality Charter, which I think is a joke; it's just based on tick the boxes. From what I've seen, universities who have got the charter haven't had to

show that they've improved opportunities for staff of colour- that doesn't seem to be part of that. I don't see improvement; I'm just seeing it getting worse especially with the global politics at the moment. Anything around racism is just going to get worse. (Interview 10)

The picture is bleak. New diversity strategies do not seriously engage with structural issues around race in the same way that they appear to do so with gender; diversity in this way can be seen as a mechanism to maintain privilege (i.e. whiteness) rather than challenge it (Ahmed 2012: 151). Within this climate it is no wonder that the advancement of racially marked academics in higher education is so dismal. Representation is a mockery when it only amounts to 'Benetton style' campaigns to desperately market the diversity of the institution. In the absence of a real commitment to structural reform around race equality this will remain the case and racially marked academics will continue to represent the few, at the bottom of the hierarchy, and unable to progress.

Conclusion

Throughout this chapter my respondents have shared their experiences of being unsupported in applications for promotion, a lack of mentoring, job insecurity, and an overwhelming sense of being undervalued. The obstacles and challenges that they have encountered in relation to hiring practices and career progression are immense, and for the most part appear impossible to overcome. I myself have experienced first hand the various barriers around career advancement and it is insulting, exhausting, and devaluing, and as also pointed out by my respondents, it is particularly frustrating when one does their due diligence to only find that they are more qualified in comparison to their white counterparts, yet they still encounter rejection. But the one thing I can say is that with the frequency of these occurrences, there is clear evidence that it is less the case that *we* are inadequate, and more the case that the institution is racist. The university is ultimately a space of whiteness that continues to cultivate whiteness as a way to ensure that the dominant culture is reproduced and maintained. It is structured by white norms and values that show no signs of shifting to a more open terrain anytime soon; the desire for such transformation is simply not there, and no amount of superficial diversity initiatives can hide this depressing reality. If racially marked academics are to feel truly valued and supported then a series of structural, intellectual, and ethical obligations, must be implemented in higher education to ensure the advancement and inclusion for all.

Notes

1. See, 'UK Study Finds Just 17 Black Female Professors,' *Independent*, 3 February 2015. https://www.independent.co.uk/student/news/uk-study-finds-just-17-black-female-professors-10019201.html.
2. See, 'Ethnic Minority Academics Earn Less Than White Colleagues,' *BBC News*, 7 December 2018. https://www.bbc.co.uk/news/education-46473269.
3. The Equality Act replaced and streamlined previous existing equality legislation safeguarding groups who fall under the nine protected characteristics (age, disability, gender reassignment, marriage and civil partnership, pregnancy and maternity, race, religion, sex, sexual orientation) from discrimination in employment, education, the provision of goods, facilities and services, the management of premises and the exercise of public functions. The Public Sector Duty requires Higher Education Institutions to publish annual information to demonstrate compliance with the equality duty. It also requires them to publish measurable objectives based on the aims of the General Duty, which seeks to eliminate harassment, advance equality and remove disadvantage, and foster good relations. For further info see, https://www.gov.uk/guidance/equality-act-2010-guidance.
4. See, Adams (2018) 'UK Universities Making Slow Progress on Equality, Data Shows,' *The Guardian,* 7 September 2018. https://www.theguardian.com/education/2018/sep/07/uk-university-professors-black-minority-ethnic.

References

Ahmed, S. (2012). *On Being Included: Racism and Diversity in Institutional Life*. Durham: Duke University Press.

Ali, M. (2015, July 21). A Study Reveals a Painful Truth Behind a Story About Chris Rock's Neighbors. *UpWorthy*. https://www.upworthy.com/a-study-reveals-a-painful-truth-behind-a-story-about-chris-rocks-neighbors.

Anderson, B. (2010). Migration, Immigration Controls and the Fashioning of Precarious Workers. *Work, Employment & Society, 24*(2), 300–317.

Bhopal, K. (2016). *The Experiences of Black and Minority Ethnic Academics: A Comparative Study of the Unequal Academy*. London: Routledge.

Binet, L. (2018). *The 7th Function of Language*. London: Vintage.

Chan, A., Dhamoon, R., & Moy, L. (2014). Metaphoric Representations of Women of Colour in the Academy: Teaching Race, Disrupting Power. *Borderlands, 13*(2), 1–26.

Croxford, R. (2018, December 7). Ethnic Minority Academics Earn Less Than White Colleagues. *BBC News*. https://www.bbc.co.uk/news/education-46473269.

Equality Challenge Unit. (2018). *Equality Charters Explained*. https://www.ecu.ac.uk/equality-charters/charter-marks-explained/.

Garner, R. (2015, February 3). UK Study Finds Just 17 Black Female Professors. *Independent*. https://www.independent.co.uk/student/news/uk-study-finds-just-17-black-female-professors-10019201.html.

Niemann, Y. (2012). Lessons from the Experiences of Women of Color Working in Academia. In G. Muhs, Y. Niemann, C. Gonzalez, & A. Harris (Eds.), *Presumed Incompetent: The Intersections of Race and Class for Women in Academia* (pp. 446–501). Boulder: University Press of Colorado.

Pilkington, A. (2013). The Interacting Dynamics of Institutional Racism in Higher Education. *Race Ethnicity and Education, 16*(2), 225–245.

Rangasamy, J. (2004). Understanding Institutional Racism: Reflections from Linguistic Anthropology. In I. Law, D. Philips, & L. Turney (Eds.), *Institutional Education in Higher Education* (pp. 27–34). Stoke on Trent: Trentham Books.

Sayyid, S. (2004). Slippery People: The Immigrant Imaginary and the Grammar of Colours. In I. Law, D. Philips, & L. Turney (Eds.), *Institutional Education in Higher Education* (pp. 149–159). Stoke on Trent: Trentham Books.

Shilliam, R. (2015). Black Academia: The Doors Have Been Opened but the Architecture Remains the Same. In C. Alexander & R. Arday (Eds.), *Aiming Higher: Race, Inequality and Diversity in the Academy* (pp. 32–35). London: Runnymede Trust.

Sian, K. (2017). Being Black in a White World: Understanding Racism in British Universities. *International Journal on Collective Identity Research, 2*(176), 1–26.

Stanley, C. (2006). Coloring the Academic Landscape: Faculty of Color Breaking the Silence in Predominantly White Colleges and Universities. *American Educational Research Journal, 43*(4), 701–736.

Thomas, G., & Hollenshead, C. (2001). Resisting from the Margins: The Coping Strategies of Black Women and Other Women of Color Faculty Members at a Research University. *The Journal of Negro Education, 70*(3), 166–175.

Wallace, D. (2018). Cultural Capital as Whiteness? Examining Logics of Ethno-Racial Representation and Resistance. *British Journal of Sociology of Education, 39*(4), 466–482.

Waring, C. (2018, August 17). Black and Biracial Americans Wouldn't Need to Code-Switch If We Lived in a Post-Racial Society. *The Conversation.* https://theconversation.com/black-and-biracial-americans-wouldnt-need-to-code-switch-if-we-lived-in-a-post-racial-society-101013.

Yosso, T. (2005). Whose Culture Has Capital? A Critical Race Theory Discussion of Community Cultural Wealth. *Race Ethnicity and Education, 8*(1), 69–91.

7

Resisting Racism in the Academy: *'Wherever We, Are We Belong'*

Introduction

The story so far has demonstrated the major challenges that racially marked academics are confronted with in the university. From their day-to-day interactions, to their experiences of teaching and career progression, the fight against racism in the academy appears unrelenting. In a climate where we are repeatedly scrutinized, monitored, undervalued, ignored, alienated, and marginalized, what are the strategies we develop to resist? Resistance against racism in higher education can take different forms for different people. For some resistance is to cope, for others it's to survive, and for some resistance is to be part of a movement that seeks to transform structures of power. No one form of resistance is more courageous than the other; each method is dependent upon the context and positioning of the individual in their institution. For racially marked, early career academics, on fixed term contracts or still on probation, resistance in an overt fashion may prove detrimental to their careers. Similarly for those on more secure contracts and those

© The Author(s) 2019   **153**
K. P. Sian, *Navigating Institutional Racism in British Universities*,
Mapping Global Racisms, https://doi.org/10.1007/978-3-030-14284-1_7

who occupy a more senior position, whilst it is true that they may have slightly more power, it does not necessarily mean that it is any easier for them to challenge whiteness.

There is a somewhat misplaced and idealistic hope that when one of us 'makes it' we are able to change the system, in fact from my observations for racially marked academics in senior management roles it is actually more testing, particularly because white colleagues and managers are often working to undermine their position of authority. We can only do what we can do subject to our context. There is perhaps an unfair tendency to think that those who make it to the top 'sell out,' and leave us behind to struggle, because understandably we put all of our hope into them to fix the problem. That's a heavy burden for anyone to carry, and I think although on the surface it might seem that they are in a very comfortable position we cannot underestimate the enormous challenges and pressures that they encounter behind closed doors, particularly as they are likely to face even more backlash and white resentment because they have managed to climb up the ladder. As such it doesn't necessarily get easier at the top, rather the monitoring and the scrutiny intensifies, because structures of whiteness are always hostile and antagonistic when a person of colour takes the throne.

Regardless of our position and the techniques that we adopt, resistance is a mechanism that helps racially marked academics to navigate hostile environments. As the chapter will go onto demonstrate acts of resistance come through the cultivation of friendships, strategic allies, and networks. The bonds that develop out of our shared experiences in the university provide for many of us an important source of strength, as Angela Davis points out, 'it is in collectivities that we find reservoirs of hope and optimism' (2016: 47). In the absence of conventional forms of guidance and mentoring, these connections allow our voices to be heard. Our grievances and anxieties can be discussed with a sympathetic ear that will listen; sometimes we just need somebody to listen. Speaking to one another about our struggles and our challenges in our institutions also allows us to realize that we are not alone, that we are not exaggerating particular incidents, and that indeed our frustrations and fears are valid. As the academy increasingly marginalizes and excludes racially marked academics, our collective groupings become crucial for providing a sense of belonging, protection and support.

Friendships and Informal Networks

As mentioned in the previous chapter racially marked academics often have to rely upon external, more informal networks of support. These are our spaces; they allow us to come together and seek advice, or sometimes just a chat is enough. These spaces are where relationships, connections, and friendships grow, as Margalynne Armstrong and Stephanie Wildman point out, 'friendship provides a space for speaking the truth about an institution, rather than supressing or silencing it' (2012: 240). These spaces represent important sites of resistance and give many racially marked academics the room to breathe and share their experiences in the comfort that they won't simply be dismissed (ibid.). They can take any shape and might include going for coffee, meeting as a more structured group, or talking over the telephone. These may appear on the surface to be very mundane acts, but the development of a space to talk, laugh, cry and let it all out can be incredibly powerful. The act of reaching out, the act of speaking, of listening, of supporting and of sharing is to fight back, defy, and persevere. My respondents spoke about the importance of these spaces and groupings in facilitating conversations, as one participant said:

> We create these ad hoc groupings with others in similar situations, but these are not formal arrangements within the institution. I found these ad hoc groupings massively important, we'd have conversations, even if nothing practical was to come out from them, to say and share what we were having to deal with was important. (Interview 14)

The development of these informal networks is key to establishing a sense of belonging, safety and solidarity for racially marked academics. They serve as an important space to help each other navigate racism and discrimination within the academy (Niemann 2012: 496–497). Another respondent commented:

> We have had to almost cultivate a hidden network of people that is completely outside our own universities. Knowing that we have that support with each other from outside is so important, it makes me feel less alone. It's like we can go to each other for help or just talk it out, it feels more like a group of friends who understand and can relate to what each other is going through. I've found that network vital for my own survival in academia. (Interview 17)

In her research on Native women in the academy, Michelle M. Jacob similarly found that her respondents spoke of the 'necessity' of having Native friends in university spaces in order to survive. There was a familiar emphasis on the significance of building collectives across universities, which serve as crucial sites of support, particularly in times of 'crisis' (2012: 247–248). She also describes the way in which her respondents stressed the importance of ensuring that such collectives are built across generations, that is, to support, guide and teach future generations of Native scholars about how to cope and potentially thrive in academic spaces (ibid.). As the next interviewee points out, these collective relationships and connections give strength and hope to racially marked academics:

> I think it's only through each other we can survive this space. It makes a statement that we can actually be in this space together. Finding each other in these spaces makes things so much better; it can save us from attrition. It allows us to occupy a space, which may have been off limits to us as individuals. (Interview 20)

Undeniably the relationships that we forge with other racially marked academics are fundamental to our survival in the academy. The connections outlined could be described as what Catherine Lu refers to as 'political friendships,' those that are, 'founded on mutual recognition and respect' (2009: 54). They offer the potential to provide an important 'enabling condition' for the formation of wider social collectives (ibid.). Lu goes onto suggest that within this sphere of friendship one can find the support 'for engaging in painful self-examinations and reflections of their past, present and future collective political selves' (ibid.: 55). The interview responses have demonstrated key elements of this type of connection whereby common experiences, a shared respect, and a wider understanding of the collective struggle, establishes long-lasting bonds and alliances.

However at the same time it is also important to address some key realities, as there is a danger that such relationships become romanticized. What I have just set out could indeed be read as falling into this very trap. While our connections are of significant importance, it would be misguided to simply suggest that conflict between racially marked academics does not exist. As Angela Harris and Carmen Gonzalez remind us, we must 'not assume that people of colour support other people of colour' (2012: 494). This may seem counter-productive in light of what has already been stated above, however, we cannot escape the realities on the ground and the environment in which we work. Due to the vast neoliberalization of the university a climate of cut-throat competition has been cultivated, whereby tendencies for what Harris and Gonzalez describe as 'crab mentality' prevail (ibid.). This refers to attempts made to bring down others in the fear that they are getting ahead (ibid.). When racially marked academics thrive and succeed there may be a sense of resentment from other racially marked academics, and there may be various back door manoeuvrings to undermine their accomplishments. These relationships would perhaps fall under the category of Lu's 'politicized friendships,' which are those that are 'driven by "rivalrous self-interest"' and 'breed political discord, conflict and enmity' (2009: 54). People of colour are not immune from adopting these positions, and do so for a range of different reasons, the point being, it is too simplistic to believe that racially marked academics will automatically support other racially marked academics.

Another concern is around the various expectations placed on racially marked academics by other racially marked academics, some of which I mentioned in the introduction to this chapter. As we start building our profiles, more requests are made for us to help other racially marked academics. While it is always important to support one another, the demands can be unrealistic and unfair, therefore we must recognize what we can and cannot do. Setting boundaries can be a way to ensure that we do not become overburdened with requests or guilt-ridden if we cannot meet particular demands. Many of us have a tendency to 'over-give,' which facilitates some taking advantage (unintentionally, for the most part). In a number of cases this occurs in our own informal networks, whereby help and support is confused with the expectation that we take on additional labour. I maintain that our connections across academia can act as key sites for empowerment, but like all social relationships they are also prone to being abused. As Essed rightly points out, 'there is a price tag to racial solidarity' (2000: 901). I believe that being aware of this is in itself an act of resistance as it allows for the development of relationships based on trust and cooperation rather than crude, and individually driven transactions.

It was clear from the interview data that just the very presence of racially marked academics in one university can be empowering for other racially marked academics in another. Although we remain few in number we are gradually infiltrating academia in more ways than ever. That shift, albeit slow, is certainly contributing to changing the face of British academia. Despite white reluctance and structural opposition to encourage this change, racially marked academics are certainly beginning to represent an exciting break from the conventional system, as one respondent said:

> I think that there are a growing number of people coming through the system who are not your typical academic. There are more women, more working class people and more people of colour, and this breaks with the traditional pale, stale academic that we tend to think of. So not only are we slowly changing the complexion of academia, but we're bringing completely new ideas and a new vocabulary. (Interview 14)

As racially marked academics continue to infiltrate the university, we are sending out a collective message that we have the power to interrupt oppressive, dominant structures of whiteness:

We need to infiltrate every level and every space and just remember that. Perhaps one of the most important messages I've ever heard is from my brother, he told me that I belong wherever I am. If we remember that whatever role we take and no matter how shit we're treated, just by being in the space we're changing it - whether we say something or not. Wherever we are we belong. (Interview 20)

Whichever way we choose to occupy the university space, just our very *being* as racially marked academics, is to transform that environment, and to transform any environment is in itself the hallmark of resistance. Building networks are key to our survival, but as already discussed, it is also important that we remain pragmatic in both what we can deliver and our own expectations. Some networks may be more ambitious than others with the potential for real growth and widespread solidarity, and if all are committed to investing in these spaces they can provide an important channel for change. On the day-to-day level, in my own experience many people come and many people go; my deeper connections and relationships with other racially marked academics therefore comprise of a tiny collective of which I can count on one hand, and who I would regard as lifelong, political friends. Our networks can therefore take varied shapes and forms and no one model is more effective than the other. Whether it's having one person or ten people to talk to, the heart of resistance lies in the creation of a sub-space where we can find acceptance, respect, and cooperation to fight against a wider landscape of exclusion and oppression.

Resisting Through *Knowing*

By virtue of *being* a person of colour, whatever environment we find ourselves within, our histories and our lived experiences will most likely (often instinctively) guide us and arm us, in a political sense, with the tools to critically engage, unpack, and question our positionality. Whether or not we choose to be 'woke,' our trajectories, as people of colour, will have some form of impact on our overall outlook. We learn through our ancestors, grandparents, and parents struggles that we were not born privileged and entitled, and although this may have never been 'officially' stated to us as youngsters, we were for the most part attuned to seeing, feeling, and hearing cries of injustice. As we piece together our histories, bit-by-bit we learn new knowledges, new ideas, and new languages to narrate our experiences and biographies. Through the art of *knowing* we become empowered, as we increasingly engage with, develop, and build upon scholarship that has provided a home, and a voice, for many of us (e.g. critical race theory, decolonial studies, critical Muslim studies, postcolonial studies, black feminism, etc.). In this sense, our conceptual tools have helped us to navigate our immediate social settings, including our places of work, as one respondent said:

> It's great that we're building a body of scholarship around these issues and we need to continue doing this. Resisting comes in our knowing. My ancestors didn't get as far as I did, and I'm using all the tools that I've learned to try and pass on that knowledge through my work, so that the next black or brown academic behind me can take it up and take it further, and eventually change the system. (Interview 20)

Our *knowing* as the participant suggests, is not just some form of abstract theorizing, but can be used and applied to make real, practical changes on the ground for future scholars of colour. Documenting, logging, and recording our experiences is thus central to the project of educating those who come after us, and in doing so provides them with the etchings of a map to be followed and built upon. Retelling our narratives and journey's is not only strategic, but also in many cases it can be cathartic and empowering. As Daniel G. Solorzano and Dolores Delgado Bernal point out, 'although the act of political writing can be a form of internal transformational resistance, once it is published or made public, it can be a very powerful form of external transformational resistance' (2001: 326). Here we should revisit bell hooks and Patricia Hill Collins to remind ourselves of the importance of resistance on the margins, through our work and our ideas. That is, to embrace and creatively use our marginality to institutionalize other ways of seeing and doing (e.g. decolonizing the curriculum) (S29–S30).

As hooks reminds us, 'our words are not without meaning, they are an action, a resistance' (1989: 16). The using of our *knowing* in such a way, as a result of our positionality, has the potential to make real shifts in the university setting, particularly as it continues to inspire and enthuse a new generation of BME scholars, as one respondent commented:

> I think the ground swell of the so-called 'undesirables' of the academic world is really making an intervention because we're loud, we don't just write for academic outlets, we engage with the media and community spaces and we're part of third sector organizations. I know we're still marginal but I think we are making change in our own ways. (Interview 14)

The participant is alluding to the notion of 'scholar-activism,' which is that which broadly refers to academics who draw upon and apply both their research and intellectual activity to the grassroots level. It is about facilitating engagement beyond the confines of the academy to build local, national and global alliances and solidarities with marginalized groups and activist organizations. Scholar-activism requires an awareness of one's positionality and privilege and seeks to proactively, and collaboratively, challenge forms of injustice and inequality (Derickson 2015: 392). Scholar-activism can be an important avenue for resistance for racially marked academics, as it enables us to recognize the value of our work and the difference (or 'impact') we make on the outside, which as we have seen is typically dismissed by our universities. It also has the power to bring more of us together and think through collectively how the various strategies and campaigns that we have been involved in on the outside, might be brought back into the academy to organize around social justice and anti-racism. The next respondent picks this up and speaks of the way in which our scholarship offers the potential to facilitate change within the academy:

> I think people of colour can resist and raise our issues and concerns through the tools we've already learned from our own work and scholarship. So applying them through writing, campaign work, through lobbying, and crafting spaces within our own institutions to talk about racism in the academy. (Interview 4)

The knowledge and skills that we have acquired, and continue to acquire, as racially marked academics, cannot and should not be under-estimated, and through both our writing and our activism we have the potential to inspire, energize, and transform. Resistance in this sense is about the ability to put our education into practice to initiate change. It is in our *knowing* that we are able to develop the conceptual and practical tools to disrupt, challenge and liberate. Here I am taken back to an interview that I conducted with Sara Ahmed a few years ago. When we discussed how to resist the various challenges in the university she said:

> Knowing whiteness and knowing about whiteness has actually given me a lens to interpret so much about how knowledge works, about how bodies work – including social bodies – and about how philosophy works…We are the new philosophers because of our experience of coming up against whiteness. I have a certain kind of optimism about what knowledge can do. The more of us that there are, hitting the wall, the more capacity we have to make connections through each other; it becomes harder for them to keep that wall up. (2014: 32)

Resistance in the academy through *knowing* gives racially marked academics a degree of power to shape knowledge production and in doing so we are able to challenge epistemological racism in our universities (Bernal 2002: 121). However, as we have seen our *knowing* does not solely refer to an intellectual project, it also entails hands-on, practical skills that we have learned from our communities, our heritage, and our experiences. Combined this offers the scope for structural change in our institutions, and that can take shape through campaign work, or through the dissemination of our writing to wider audiences. On a smaller scale it is about having the tools to, at the very least, recognize that how the system that we work within is patterned by unequal power relations. This recognition means that we are not blind to the inequality that currently structures our universities, and the very act of acknowl-edging this is to resist its hegemonic discourses and practices. It is in this way that our knowledge becomes power.

On White Allies

Within the university environment, friends, colleagues, and 'coalitions' can play a significant role for racially marked academics (Armstrong and Wildman 2012: 240). White allies represent those who have both recognized and critiqued the privilege attached to their whiteness (Niemann 2012: 451). They are aware of their power, yet will use their positioning and expertise to support racially marked academics. They may actually 'lose credibility' from their white co-workers, who may no longer regard them as 'objective' (Armstrong and Wildman 2012: 240). They may hold different views and opinions, but if they remain supportive and a sense of trust is established, white allies can be a tremendous source of support for racially marked academics (ibid.). That said racially marked academics are at risk if they are perceived to 'rely' or 'depend' too much upon white allies, these wider racist assumptions may undermine them and, "reinforce the presumption of incompetence" (ibid.). A strong white ally is somebody who recognizes whiteness, rather than simply being aware of race when an academic of colour enters the room (ibid.). It is the recognition of one's privilege and helping to establish a more equal and just environment.

A weak white ally or what I will describe as a white frenemy, is somebody who exploits our experiences for their own personal gain, for example using our 'ethnic experiences' to co-write a paper to which we are placed as second author. This is an all too common occurrence that has long existed in the social sciences, whereby white researchers seek to 'buddy up' with racially marked academics, only to subject their personal experiences to crude, Orientalist, positivist measurements. The experiences of the 'other' (often unintentionally corroborated by a racially marked academic) are thus capitalized upon to serve white gain, white fame, and white career driven interests. For too long racially marked academics have had to endure being either 'subjects' of research, or (frustrated) onlookers of those who continue to profit from the experiences of marginalized communities at the local and global level, in a superficial name-building exercise. Those guilty of perpetuating these forms of research need to reflect deeply upon their praxis and narcissism before claiming that they are 'experts' in the field.

A white frenemy is also somebody who thinks it's 'cool' to have a black or brown friend, and goes on to parade us to their colleagues. They are the ones who promise to help us but never actually follow through; they lecture us on the importance of social justice, however when they are confronted with racial injustice in their own institutions they remain silent. White frenemies will often work to undermine racially marked academics, as they are not committed to structural change; they actively perpetuate discourses of whiteness to maintain their position of power. In short, the white frenemy does not want to risk losing their privilege and the benefits such privilege generates.

In my own experience, I have come across a few white colleagues who I would certainly describe as allies/friends. The support has come in many ways, from writing strong references, sharing CVs, reading over-written work, putting my name forward for particular opportunities, informal mentoring, displays of solidarity, and most of all being a confidante. Those who have gone further have committed themselves to developing and implementing anti-racist policies and practices even when challenged by those in senior management positions. These various acts of allyship represent those who have (to paraphrase Les Back) 'reckoned with whiteness' (2004: 4). My respondents spoke about the importance of having white allies, for example one participant said:

> Some white members of the academy have done extraordinary things for people of colour, so cultivating positions or a climate where it's viable that people of colour are competitive for various positions, or ensuring that they find a footing in senior positions. And all this is important, it is necessary for our growth and sense of belonging. (Interview 18)

This was picked up by another respondent who also recognized the value of white allyship:

> It's certainly good to have, and find, white allies, because sometimes you get to tap into whatever social capital is available to you, and that's important because we're all negotiating power. But they're one person. We have to try and convert more and more people as we go. And then slowly

we build a network of allies, but we always, always need the energy to do that in addition to everything that we're doing. (Interview 20)

As alluded to above, while white allyship is important there is a clear lack of opportunity to actually develop such relationships within university spaces. Furthermore, in most instances, cultivating those connections is often the outcome of our labour, and the energy that we invest. For the vast majority of my respondents, they had very little exposure to, and experience of, white allyship, which is suggestive of the rarity of this form of support. While white allies offer racially marked academics support, it remains crucially important to also recognize that the work involved in creating a fair environment should not rest solely upon their shoulders, but rather it should be the minimum requirement of all of our white co-workers. As Armstrong and Wildman argue at the very least, 'all whites have a stake in workplace fairness, anti-bias, and non-discrimination' (2012: 240). They go onto suggest that:

Being an observant co-worker, speaking out against observed oppression, and seeking to ensure workplace fairness for everyone may lead to friendship...Friends do not deny the reality that another experiences; rather they learn about themselves from their friend's perspective. Colour insight provides a tool to deepen the insights that co-workers of friends may gain from each other. (ibid.)

Barnor Hesse (2016) gives us an important critical insight into the logics of whiteness, which is particularly useful here in order to understand the different positionalities that our white colleagues may adopt in the university (and beyond) in their (non)showing of solidarity. In his development of '8 White Identities,'[1] Hesse argues that there is a regime of whiteness constituted by a set of action-oriented white identities. Those who identify with whiteness (both whites and non-whites) typically fall into the following categories, defined by Hesse as:

1. **White Supremacist**: Preserves, names, and values white superiority.
2. **White Voyeurism**: Would not challenge a white supremacist; desires non-whiteness because it is interesting, pleasurable; seeks to control the consumption and appropriation of non-whiteness; fascination

with culture (ex: consuming Black culture without the burden of Blackness).

3. **White Privilege**: May critique white supremacy, but maintains a deep investment in questions of fairness/equality under the normalization of whiteness and white rule; sworn goal of 'diversity.'

4. **White Benefit**: Sympathetic to a set of issues but only privately. Will not speak/act in solidarity publicly, because they are benefitting through whiteness in public (some People of Colour are in this category too).

5. **White Confessional**: Some exposure of whiteness takes place, but as a way of being accountable to People of Colour after; seek validation from People of Color.

6. **White Critical**: Take on board critiques of whiteness and invest in exposing/marking the white regime; refuses to be complicit with the regime; whiteness speaking back to whiteness.

7. **White Traitor**: Actively refuses complicity; names what is going on; intention is to subvert white authority and tell the truth at whatever cost; need them to dismantle institutions.

8. **White Abolitionist**: Changes institutions; dismantling whiteness, and not allowing whiteness to reassert itself.

I would suggest that the book has demonstrated enough evidence to show that the first 5 categories are perhaps the most hegemonic positions adopted by largely white staff members in British universities. Throughout the book we have seen a mix of cases ranging from direct harassment, cultural appropriation/Orientalism, to more 'liberal' or post-racial approaches that seek to deny and mask the institutional nature of racism, while superficially championing diversity. All the common experiences shared by those interviewed strongly indicate that the level of critical white colleagues in our universities is extremely limited, often non-existent. As I have outlined above, in my own experiences I have been fortunate to cross paths with a few white allies during my time in academia, these certainly fulfill the criteria for the white critical, and in some cases the white traitor, in even fewer cases, the white abolitionist. If our white colleagues are serious about showing solidarity and support, they must seek to adopt categories 6–8. In doing so they are demonstrating that they are willing to both use and critique their privilege as a way to dismantle racism at any cost. Categories 7 and 8 are perhaps the least adopted even by those who might be considered more critical, precisely because they depend upon the relinquishing of one's benefits and require action.

White allies (whether white criticals, white traitors, or white abolitionists) are undeniably important sources of support for racially marked academics. However, as long as universities continue to construct and reproduce whiteness as the norm, these acts of solidarity will be of marginal significance (Sian 2017: 18). To form meaningful resistance against racism in the academy our white colleagues must recognize their own role in perpetuating whiteness, they must critically reflect upon their privilege, and they must actively organize and commit to embedding structural changes that seek to abolish racism. In doing so an environment that benefits all can not only be envisioned but also actualized.

Conclusion

People of colour are remarkably strong. Our ancestors have endured and fought tirelessly against centuries of racist violence and oppression, laying down the foundations for a better future for us, and the next generations. Those structures of racism have of course persisted throughout the West and continue to shape our contemporary condition. Because of our *knowing*, strength and courage are baked into our souls. We are well aware early on that the world that we will come to inhabit is not one of privilege, pampering, and entitlement, but one of resilience and hope. In the university space, racially marked academics are often involved in complex negotiations around how they might resist racism in the academy. Resistance is subject to one's context and capacities, thus tactics can range from fight back, organizing, writing, finding support, sharing, perseverance, and survival. Whether we choose to be assertive or strategic, and develop a collective or an individual response, we must carefully consider the possibility of exercising our agency. Resisting a hegemonic politics of whiteness is challenging and exhausting, and can take its toll on our physical and mental well-being. Whichever method we choose to adopt in our resistance against racism in the academy, it is important that we remember that we are (both intentionally and unintentionally) engaging in a larger global struggle against white supremacy.

This chapter has demonstrated most clearly that when we are able to share with others our experiences, we are all the stronger for doing so. This takes away the sense of isolation and paranoia, it also allows us to speak about our challenges and anxieties with those who understand, who will listen, and who will support. We have seen the strength and the potential of collective resistance, as well as some of the realities of political/politicized friendships. The importance of documenting our journeys was also highlighted as a way to show the power and creativity that can come from our shared, lived experiences in the academy. We looked to the value of scholar-activism for developing wider networks of solidarity and the possibility of applying the lessons that we have learned from the outside back into our places of work. The final part of the chapter sought to address the potential for developing white allies, considering in some detail how they might facilitate institutional changes, if of course they are willing to dismantle their privilege first.

It is evident that we are agents rather than victims of the racist structure within which we work. Throughout the course of researching this book and speaking to all the inspiring and courageous racially marked academics, it's clear that together we have the ability to represent a vehicle for change so long as we are driven by a collective spirit, rather than individualistic objectives; after all, 'one needs a community of resistance' (hooks 1989: 19). It is in this togetherness that we can continue to cultivate political friendships and help one another see that *wherever we are, we belong…*

Note

1. Hesse, B. (2016, November 10). Available at: https://twitter.com/barnor_hesse/status/796784744591724544.

References

Ahmed, S. (2014). Sara Ahmed. In K. Sian (Ed.), *Conversations in Postcolonial Thought* (pp. 15–33). London: Palgrave Macmillan.

Armstrong, M., & Wildman, S. (2012). Working Across Racial Lines in a Not-So-Post-Racial World. In G. Muhs, Y. Niemann, C. Gonzalez, & A. Harris (Eds.), *Presumed Incompetent: The Intersections of Race and Class for Women in Academia* (pp. 224–241). Boulder: University Press of Colorado.

Back, L. (2004). Ivory Towers? The Academy and Racism. In I. Law, D. Phillips, & L. Turney (Eds.), *Institutional Racism in Higher Education* (pp. 1–6). Staffordshire: Trentham Books.

Bernal, D. (2002). Critical Race Theory, Latino Critical Theory, and Critical Raced-Gendered Epistemologies: Recognizing Students of Color as Holders and Creators of Knowledge. *Qualitative Inquiry, 8*(1), 105–126.

Davis, A. (2016). *Freedom Is a Constant Struggle*. Chicago: Haymarket Books.

Derickson, K. (2015). Situated Solidarities and the Practice of Scholar-Activism. *Environment and Planning D: Society and Space, 33*(3), 391–407.

Essed, P. (2000). Dilemmas in Leadership: Women of Colour in the Academy. *Ethnic and Racial Studies, 23*(5), 888–904.

Harris, A., & Gonzalez, C. (2012). Lessons from the Experiences of Women of Colour Working in Academia. In G. Muhs, Y. Niemann, C. Gonzalez, & A. Harris (Eds.), *Presumed Incompetent: The Intersections of Race and Class for Women in Academia* (pp. 446–504). Boulder: University Press of Colorado.

Hesse, B. (2016, November 10). Available at: https://twitter.com/barnor_hesse/status/796784744591724544.

hooks, b. (1989). Choosing the Margin as a Space of Racial Openness. *The Journal of Cinema and Media, 36,* 15–23.

Jacob, M. (2012). Native Women Maintaining Their Culture in the White Academy. In G. Muhs, Y. Niemann, C. Gonzalez, & A. Harris (Eds.), *Presumed Incompetent: The Intersections of Race and Class for Women in Academia* (pp. 446–501). Boulder: University Press of Colorado.

Lu, C. (2009). Political Friendship Among Peoples. *Journal of International Political Theory, 5*(1), 41–58.

Niemann, Y. (2012). Lessons from the Experiences of Women of Color Working in Academia. In G. Muhs, Y. Niemann, C. Gonzalez, & A. Harris (Eds.), *Presumed Incompetent: The Intersections of Race and Class for Women in Academia* (pp. 446–501). Boulder: University Press of Colorado.

Sian, K. (2017). Being Black in a White World: Understanding Racism in British Universities. *International Journal on Collective Identity Research, 176*(2), 1–26.

Solorzano, G., & Bernal, D. (2001). Examining Transformational Resistance Through a Critical Race and Latcrit Theory Framework: Chicana and Chicano Students in an Urban Context. *Urban Education, 36*(3), 308–342.

8

Looking Ahead: Recommendations for Policy and Practice

In 2002, Laura Turney, Ian Law and Deborah Phillips developed an anti-racist toolkit to address institutional racism in higher education. It came as a critical response following the Macpherson Report (1999) and built a set of conceptual and methodological tools to both embed racial equality in higher education, and ensure a long-term commitment to anti-racist politics in the university (2002: 93–103). The toolkit recognized that all of the institution's operations would in some way impact upon the experiences of racially marked staff and students, and therefore called for universities to identify, reflect and act upon the key areas where discrimination may arise (ibid: 94–95). Emphasizing the responsibilities and obligations that the university has to the promotion of race equality, the authors developed a theoretical, legal, and practical framework, to address racism in the academy. They pointed to the way in which institutional racism, Eurocentrism, and whiteness structured most higher education institutions, and introduced notions of accountability in relation to race equality policy and anti-racist practice (ibid.: 98). The toolkit addressed fundamental areas including the monitoring of employment practices, student recruitment, teaching and learning, research, contracts and purchasing, and external affairs. The toolkit

© The Author(s) 2019
K. P. Sian, *Navigating Institutional Racism in British Universities*,
Mapping Global Racisms, https://doi.org/10.1007/978-3-030-14284-1_8

has been widely disseminated giving universities the opportunity to review and evaluate their operations and practices. However, despite these important interventions, the broader climate has increasingly sought to dilute race equality in all sectors of society (Sian et al. 2013: 51–77). This has meant that public, political and organizational commitments to anti-racism have gradually collapsed.

Well over a decade on from the development of the toolkit, we are still faced with the stark under-representation of racially marked academics, as institutional racism engulfing the academy appears to show very little sign of abating. These issues and concerns continue to be researched and documented with the same sets of arguments being raised about racism in the university. This book therefore sits within the existing extensive literature on the topic, and further supports and evidences the prevalence of racism in higher education. Through its collaboration with a range of racially marked academics, this work has once again identified that we collectively experience persistent forms of racism through a lack of institutional support, difficulties around teaching and curriculum design, barriers to career advancement, and day-to-day racism. When I asked my participants what they felt needed to be done in order to address racism in universities, the message was overwhelmingly clear: racism is a widespread, structural issue within universities, and measures need to be implemented in a systematic way to ensure greater representation, fairer hiring practices and equal treatment at all levels. They also called for race to be put on the agenda and race equality matters to be taken seriously. Below details the key points and areas that my respondents felt needed to be addressed with urgency.

Lets Talk About Race

The liberal, colour-blind, post-racial discourse that currently organizes British universities has created an environment in which practices of racism and discrimination are deemed infrequent, occasional and uncommon. The popularization of this narrative across Britain—both by its people and its institutions—has allowed for the gradual dismantling of race equality (Sian et al. 2013: 72–74). As identified at the start of the book, such liberal articulations of racism have meant that structural forms of racism have been masked and dismissed by university management. Critical of this shift my respondents called for race to be put back on the agenda in the academy, that is the disavowal of racism can no longer be sustained, as one participant described:

> We need to change institutional structures and cultures, where discursively and interpersonally there is a full recognition that racism is a problem. Universities need to start with that basic recognition, that basic act of good faith, that people are experiencing it, and their response to it should not be condescending. (Interview 18)

The notion that a 'basic recognition' of racism was required by universities beyond lip service, was also stressed by another respondent who said:

> Universities need to have a proper conversation about racism and decolonizing education, so recognizing the traditions that have been normalized in the disciplines, but also integrating different voices. I think we need to look at black colleges in the United States. I know a lot of them are conservative in their approaches, but they are able to have a lot more control in terms of their curriculum, over who they appoint and so on- is there something that we can learn from that, which can be translated over here? I'd like to see a nationwide black scholars network, which can be used to share our experiences and think about how we can move forward. (Interview 14)

My participants are fundamentally calling for universities to invest within practical, structural changes that will facilitate real transformation on the ground. The next interviewee raises the point that issues around racism should not be left solely for those from racially marked backgrounds to deal with. He also suggests that it is up to senior managers to take the initiative to deal with their practices of racism, rather than that burden being placed upon racially marked academics. Like the above responses, he similarly argues that racism should no longer be a 'taboo' issue in the academy:

It's not the responsibility of BME people to deal with racism; it's a white problem. What are they going to do to address racism? It's something that they need to answer, rather than it falling on our shoulders time and time again. We need to take the taboo away from race in the university environment. (Interview 9)

The erasing of the commitment to anti-racism in British universities has meant that debates seeking to address racial discrimination and disadvantage are side-lined. The following response highlights some concerns around this worrying direction, whereby the participant argues that the increasing exclusion of racially marked academics and students, facilitates the further marginalization of discussions, and strategies to address racism:

Universities are meant to be spaces of critical learning, but I think they're filled with more and more white gatekeepers, 'professionals' and 'experts' who are less interested in critical scholarship, and more interested in power rather than tackling issues like racism. These people tend to inform the management of these institutions and often stifle more critical voices and debates on racism. I think universities are going in an increasingly worrying direction, they're betraying its tradition, and increasing tuition fees means that more and more BME people are being cut out not only from the space, but also the wider debate to actually change things. (Interview 14)

Universities can no longer afford to perpetuate the post-racial imaginary by denying the prevalence of racism. Such denial works to reproduce dangerous notions that race no longer matters, that it has already been dealt with, and that it no longer needs to be on the table. By clinging to this discourse, senior managers are not only revealing that they do not take racism seriously, but also that they wish to actively maintain systems of racial inequality, rather than dismantle them. The interviews throughout this book have explicitly shown that race does matter, and it continues to unfairly condition the experiences of racially marked subjects in the academy. Universities must commit to having an open, honest conversation about their embedded practices that reproduce and reaffirm disadvantage, they also need to ensure that anti-racism is central to their discourse, their practices and their politics. Only when they confront racism, can effective strategies be developed to eliminate it.

Representation and Employment Practices

My respondents were all united in their disappointment and anger around the under-representation of racially marked academics. They were all aware that despite various 'diversity drives' universities across Britain had categorically failed to address unfair employment practices, particularly around appointments, decision-making processes, and career progression. Every single one of my respondents stated that hiring committees/procedures needed to be fairer, for example:

> I think higher education needs to commit to having more representation, and it's not just representation for our own sake, but it's about who is your student intake? And this really does start to matter. I think this has a particular onus on urban universities where it is blatantly the case that they are getting a generation, which is increasingly non-white in its demographic structure. Hiring committees therefore need to be fairer to ensure these students actually have role models or senior people that look like them in the university. (Interview 18)

The next respondent argues that in order to improve representation, hiring and promotion practices need to be reviewed to ensure that they encourage racially marked academics in all aspects of their careers:

> There is a problem with things like under-representation, and the university needs to recognize that diversity does bring benefits in different ways of thinking and perceiving. You can rectify that with hiring and promotion. If we want more academics of colour in these spaces, we need to support them more throughout their PhDs. I think bias in universities is already bad, but at the senior management level it's so much worse, which is where I feel we hit the biggest barriers. (Interview 17)

This issue was picked up by another interviewee who argued that the university must take a direct, hands-on approach, to ensure that more racially marked academics occupy roles and positions within senior management:

> I think we need to start employing more people of colour for starters, and I'm not talking just about academic positions either. I'm talking about positions within senior management, because I feel like if the direction from the top doesn't entail a tone of colour, I feel like we're going to be constantly banging our heads against a brick wall, and no one on the top is going to appreciate or accept particular realities for us lot on the bottom level. So I think the university needs to make a proactive effort in order to ensure that there is representation at the very top and senior levels, and it's not because people of colour are not qualified, it's because people of colour are not given the chance, and I think there are enough studies out there to point to that. (Interview 4)

All of my respondents agreed that the simple act of changing and improving hiring practices in universities could go a long way in tackling the very real crisis around under-representation and racial inequality. The next respondent also makes the argument that this can no longer mean a purely superficial gesture in the shape of a diversity statement on job applications, but rather through audits and initiatives similar to affirmative action:

> I think racism is definitely embedded within the university, but I do still think it can be reformed. Universities require a whole audit of this problem. I think we need some form of affirmative action, this works as a recognition of institutional racism. The only thing universities currently do, is at the bottom of a job application they have some statement saying that we encourage applications from BME people, but that's purely tokenistic. (Interview 14)

This sentiment was reflected by another participant who argued:

> I think some form of affirmative action would be an important step in increasing BME participation, the only downside is that black academics would be confronted with the accusation that they're only there due to affirmative action. But having said that, that's the case for black academics

now, we're still told that we're only there to fulfil diversity agendas. This would have to be accompanied with other changes, like changes in the curriculum, changes in how we think about academia, its got to be the whole package. (Interview 12)

Universities must pledge to challenge the issue of under-representation of racially marked academics. They must systematically re-evaluate their current employment practices to ensure that hiring committees and decision-making processes at all levels, are fair and transparent. Senior managers ought to be ashamed and embarrassed by the fact that in 2018, only 1% of those from racially marked backgrounds held top positions in universities across Britain. The data continues to expose these figures year after year, the question remains then why has nothing changed? This scandal needs to be addressed and structural measures need to be implemented to make sure that once and for all, academics from racially marked backgrounds are represented fairly within the academy.

Structural Support, Recognition, and Critical Reflection

Unsurprisingly all of my respondents saw the issue of racial disadvantage in the academy as a deeply structural problem requiring institutional reform. They argued that the functioning and operations of the university were systemically racist, therefore the institution as a whole needs to be transformed. This includes the embedding of support structures for racially marked academics, the recognition of racism, and most importantly the implementation of anti-racist policy and practice, as one respondent said:

There is no support for ethnic minorities particularly at the start. I think mentoring is so important. There needs to be some acknowledgement that these issues are happening, because while there's been some recognition of gender there hasn't been on race and that's frustrating. I think it becomes problematic when diversity is used to promote the university and this happens time and time again, so it becomes less about improving structural issues or academic or student experiences, and more about the promotion of the university. I don't see change happening, not in the same way that gender or even class is acknowledged. We are so in few numbers. This work has to be done by the institution rather than the individual. (Interview 16)

The next participant makes some important, practical suggestions to improve the current situation, calling for quotas, stronger mentoring, race equality as a standing item in departmental meetings, and more support from the University and College Union (UCU). Fundamentally he is calling for a collective investment of all those involved in the university to develop and build the changes that will facilitate the creation of an anti-racist university:

> I think race equality issues should appear as regular agenda items in staff team meetings. Put race on the agenda because for so many years it hasn't been on the agenda. We need quotas. At the national level UCU should be campaigning more vigorously about this issue, I think they don't invest enough on this issue, it has to be much stronger in terms of issues around race and issues of recruitment. They make good noises occasionally but we need more national leadership over these issues. It would also help if there were more senior members invested in mentoring academics of colour. (Interview 13)

Another interviewee argued that the ideology—the institutional culture of racism—needed to change if any progress was to be made:

> Getting staff in those top positions is great and we need to do it, but we need to change the ideology, it's ideology that's keeping everyone down. It's the saddest thing to accept that if you're not white, you're not getting anywhere and all those skills we have aren't good enough. (Interview 10)

The book has demonstrated throughout that universities are structured by discourses of whiteness which work to persistently exclude racially marked academics. Universities must therefore embed alternative, multicultural frameworks that not only recognize and celebrate diversity, but also those which embed anti-racist policies and practices that take into full consideration the particularities of racially marked staff (and students). Such measures need to ensure that they offer routes for access and participation; that they accommodate the needs and demands of racially marked academics; and that a fair and equitable environment is normalized whereby difference is respected, not denigrated (Sian et al. 2013).

The following respondent calls for the same sets of important day-to-day structural changes around recruitment, mentoring, and monitoring. He also comments upon the importance of making changes to the curriculum to disrupt the centrality of Westerncentric/Eurocentric/Englishcentric knowledge productions that currently dominate British universities. He alludes to the fact that because universities are so closely bound to race and racism, perhaps the solution is to start over:

> In terms of day-to-day changes, we need to monitor our recruitment practices, improve mentoring systems and look closely at who is and who is not promoted. I also think universities need to invest in changing the curriculum, reading lists, and reimagining the canons and disciplines we're working in. There's still the embedded idea that intellectual thought is the preserve of whiteness- perhaps even Englishness. It's so deep-rooted, if intellectualism is so embedded in whiteness then all the university can do is reflect and perpetuate this. Until we radically change the way we think about intellectualism it's going to be difficult to change the way the university operates. Part of me thinks that because universities are so tied up with race and racism, which are so deeply embedded within their structures, that we need to start again. (Interview 12)

Universities must critically reflect upon their institutional values, codes, and principles, if they are serious about abolishing current patterns of racism and inequality that are swamping the sector. They need to think carefully about the outward facing message that they are presenting not only nationally but also at the global level. The continued perpetuation of insular thought and practice is no longer appealing in a fast changing global landscape. Without the willingness of senior management to take a lead in implementing these changes, the depressing, stagnant context, as documented throughout this book, will continue to be reproduced to no end.

The outlook however does not have to be this gloomy, if of course senior managers commit to leading nationwide initiatives and campaigns to stamp out racism in universities. This has to be a commitment that recognizes racism as a fundamentally structural issue, one that engages with strategies around widening participation to improve access for disadvantaged communities, and one that works with racially marked academics and students (including those who are classified as international) to ensure that their needs are being addressed appropriately. For too long, racially marked academics have been absent from the conversation, we need to feel like we are included within the debate and that our voices matter. The day-to-day racist operations of the university need to be systematically reviewed, and the failures need to be addressed seriously. Race equality must be practiced in the academy, not just preached, that is, there needs to be a clear and obvious commitment to understanding and identifying the key issues, and implementing strategies to embed the change that is required. Those of us from racially marked backgrounds working and studying within British universities are quite simply fed up of the racism that we continue to endure on a daily basis. Senior managers need to take our experiences into consideration and take the necessary action to guarantee that the university will no longer be complicit in the perpetuation of white supremacy. Only then can the vision of an anti-racist university be actualized.

Key Recommendations

- Race equality needs to be on the agenda in every department across every university in Britain. Management committee meetings must report on these issues as a standing item to demonstrate the work that they are doing to tackle institutional racism.
- University and departmental policies on race equality need to be formally reviewed and updated on an annual basis.
- Senior management need to set annual targets to increase BME representation. To ensure this process is formalized, they must implement a systematic monitoring unit to measure hiring rates of BME staff and student admissions against targets. Regular audits of the data must be made available to all staff, and failure to meet quotas will result in penalties.

- It must be made mandatory that at least one academic of colour is present on hiring committees and shortlisting panels.
- Mentoring schemes for new and current BME staff members need to be formalized, and they should be partnered with a colleague who is sensitive, and fully committed to supporting their needs around career progression and personal development.
- Clear university and departmental policies on racial harassment must be circulated regularly, to ensure that both staff and students of colour are fully aware of the routes to report and file complaints.
- Bi-annual compulsory training for staff and students on race equality must be performed.
- To ensure safe teaching and departmental spaces, a clear policy on student behaviour towards staff of colour, emphasizing zero-tolerance on racism, must be implemented and circulated to all.
- Formal training on leadership must be delivered as a key requirement for BME staff to ensure their progression into senior management roles.
- All social events for staff and students must be racially and religiously inclusive and cater for diverse needs.
- Senior managers must actively promote the research of BME staff members and research students.
- Under no circumstances can lecture capture be used by senior management as a tool to monitor, surveil and penalize the teaching delivered by racially marked academics.
- Promotions committees must take equality issues into special consideration for BME applicants.
- A commitment to decolonizing the curriculum must be led by university management to ensure that it is embedded institutionally.
- University unions need to commit to more campaign work and action around institutional racism in British universities.
- Senior management must take into account race bias and prejudice when reviewing student feedback.
- An independent ombudsman must be established that can properly investigate racist and other discriminatory practices of the university.

This book has brought to light the collective nature of the struggles that racially marked academics encounter in higher education. Its contribution lies in its findings, which raise a number of important practical and conceptual issues around racism in British universities. It has demonstrated that as a consequence of embedded practices of institutional racism (and sexism), female and male racially marked academics, at all career levels, experience emotional and psychological strain across every aspect of their profession, including in their daily interactions with colleagues, in their teaching practice, and in their chances of career progression (Sian 2017: 1–26). The findings have illustrated that there is limited support and mentoring available for racially marked academics, which works to fundamentally exclude them from the system. They are made to feel like they are invisible, that they do not belong, and that they are of no value to their institutions. They are ridiculed, harassed, belittled and ignored, experiencing sustained feelings of marginalization and non-belonging (ibid.). If these issues are to be addressed effectively, British universities need to accept that racism is endemic in higher education and can no longer be ignored. Practically, this means prioritizing the challenge to tackle racism in education, and a renewed commitment from the sector to adopt anti-racist measures that embed equality, fairness and inclusivity.

The findings of this book also point to the need for universities to provide clear access to paths for progression to ensure that racially marked academics can fully engage within the sector and realize their potential (Sian et al. 2013: 56–59). To understand the root causes of the persistent position of disadvantage experienced by racially marked academics, a dialogue is required around institutional racism, Eurocentric knowledge production, and the impact of structures of whiteness. Although much of this work is already starting to take place on the ground with important debates opened up by 'Why is my Curriculum White?' these initiatives need to be implemented at all levels of the university structure. For meaningful anti-racist practice, senior managers must develop the strategies as outlined above, which encourage and facilitate the active participation of racially marked academics into universities across Britain (Sian 2017: 1–26). In the absence of these institutional mechanisms, the possibility of social transformation in higher education is unlikely.

References

Law, I., Phillips, D., & Turney, L. (2002). Tackling Institutional Racism in Higher Education: An Antiracist Toolkit. In I. Law, D. Phillips, & L. Turney (Eds.), *Institutional Racism in Higher Education* (pp. 1–6). Staffordshire: Trentham Books.

Sian, K. (2017). Being Black in a White World: Understanding Racism in British Universities. *International Journal on Collective Identity Research, 176*(2), 1–26.

Sian, K., Law, I., & Sayyid, B. (2013). *Racism, Governance and Public Policy: Beyond Human Rights*. London: Routledge.

9

Conclusion: Backlash Blues

In the words of bell hooks:

> This is an intervention. A message from that space in the margin that is
> a site of creativity and power, that inclusive space where we recover our-
> selves, where we move in solidarity to erase the category colonised/colon-
> iser. Marginality as a site of resistance. Enter that space. Let us meet there.
> Enter that space. We greet you as liberators. (hooks 1989: 23)

This call to arms could act as inspiration for this book enabling me to
comprehend the various challenges and complexities of the academy, and
consider how we can construct solidarity and inclusion in an exclusionary institution. The pace at which universities have succumbed to brutal
neoliberal practices is startling. In 2017 university staff members and students took a stand against on-going disputes over pensions. The strikes
of 2017 however were about much more than pension cuts. Underlying
the issue was a deeper stand to call out the dire situation that has increasingly come to engulf the university sector (Sian 2017). I argued back
then that the current state of higher education is no longer sustainable as marketization, extortionate tuition fees, and impossible management demands have gradually destroyed the love for our craft (ibid.).[1]

© The Author(s) 2019   **185**
K. P. Sian, *Navigating Institutional Racism in British Universities*,
Mapping Global Racisms, https://doi.org/10.1007/978-3-030-14284-1_9

This book does not dismiss or undermine the struggles that all academics are currently facing in British universities. I am fully aware of many other widespread issues that lurk behind the walls of the university, including systematic sexual harassment, disability hate, discrimination against LGBTQIA+ communities, the toxic monitoring of Muslims under the government's Prevent duty, the on-going exploitation of international students, mental health issues, grade inflation, and the list goes on and on, and on.

I am aware that all early career academics struggle to get a foot in the door after sending out their hundreds of applications, I understand that competition is the new normal in our universities, and I can identify with the challenges of unmanageable workloads, working day and night, seven days a week on insecure contracts (ibid.). As the university has been transformed into a ruthless corporation, I have seen the way in which we have become 'service providers' for our 'student-paying-customers.' For all of us concerned, this shift is not only untenable but it is also deeply saddening, frightening and humiliating, moreover, when managers assure us about 'work-life balance' it seems like a cruel joke (ibid.). Our well-being is compromised on a daily basis, and as we battle through our anxiety, we have no choice but to put our personal life on the back burner, having to accept the fact that day in and day out our bodies and minds are exhausted (ibid.). I am sympathetic to our shared struggles as academics, and while I do not seek to neglect the various, collective issues that we are all coming up against, it is still important to recognize that in the most challenging of climates people of colour often get hit the hardest (Gillborn 2013: 481), this has been particularly true during times of economic recession or shifts in the political environment.

As the university has transformed over the years, one thing has remained un-shifting and permanent: institutional racism. There is an extensive literature on the topic that pre-dates the new boom of research documenting racism in the academy.[2] It seems racism in British universities is unchanging, with very little improvement, or progress made year after year. The new research being conducted around this issue is significantly important as it adds more and more voices across the country to strengthen the debate, which continues to expose the widespread nature of racism in the academy.[3] This book as such has positioned itself as one that contributes to theoretical, methodological, and practical interventions around racism and higher education. It is one that has been driven by the attempt to centre the voices of those academics so often left isolated, on the margins. It shares our narratives and our experiences, and by drawing upon the personal it allows us to shed light on the systemic. Moreover, it is through the empirical that the conceptual critique is enabled, which demonstrates the centrality of race in shaping and conditioning both the affective and the structural navigations of racially marked academics.

The book has been framed around key themes arising from our shared experiences. I detailed extensively the everyday microaggressions that racially marked academics encounter, but rather than simply brushing these off as a matter of a few bad colleagues, I sought to contextualize them within the wider workings of whiteness, the post-racial, and institutional racism. That is, the book has made no attempt to individualize instances of racism, rather it has shown the contrary, the embedded nature of racism, that cannot be simply reduced to a few incidents, but instead that which is symptomatic of a much larger issue of institutional racism. We went onto see how the teaching space perpetuates further challenges for racially marked academics, and how they are often confronted with challenging situations within the classroom. This led us to think about decolonizing the curriculum as a way to encourage and enhance spaces of learning that promote diversity, inclusion and anti-racism. Following on from this we saw the various barriers and difficulties that racially marked academics encounter in terms of promotion and career advancement giving texture, voice, and context, to those familiar depressing statistics around under-representation. The book went on to address the different forms of resistance that we may adopt, and the different shapes that such resistance may take. Finally, the book outlined various recommendations around how we might tackle racism effectively in the academy.

This book has been cathartic and at times difficult to write. I have been uplifted by the strength of my participants, who have since writing this book gone onto take different paths. Some have left the country to work at other universities, some have left the sector entirely, others have changed institutions, and some have stayed put. Through the daily trials and tribulations that we have all encountered, it is empowering to see that we have, and we will continue to survive the white academy. And perhaps at the very heart of the question of what it means to navigate racism in British universities, is that which denotes simply having the tools to survive, and with those tools the strength to resist.

A Final Word to My Friends

> What kept me sane was knowing that things would change, and it was a question of keeping myself together until they did. (Simone 2003: 167)

In all sectors of employment, people of colour continue to encounter rejection. This text doesn't seek to exceptionalize the role of the academy, for data consistently shows us that people of colour are unable to climb to the top of the ladder in the corporate sector, the judicial service, the political sphere, publishing, media, and the arts to name but a few. The experiences of Nina Simone have continued to fascinate me. Although actual details are unclear, Simone was allegedly denied admission into the Curtis Institute of Music to pursue her training as a classical pianist. Her dream of becoming the first female black American classical pianist, which she had been aspiring and working towards for most of her life, appeared to have fallen apart. In one interview Simone said, 'I didn't understand why I didn't get that scholarship… And there were people around me who knew about my talent as well, and they said, "Nina, it's because you are black"' (Light 2017: 39). This experience exposed Simone to the institutional practices of racism that were not only apparent in classical music, but also in mainstream America itself (ibid.: 40). Although her first love was classical music, her experiences of rejection combined with the wider political landscape of the civil rights movement, appeared to shape her later music, which took on a variety of labels including jazz, gospel, soul, and protest song. Neither in the elite domain of classical music, nor fully accepted by the mainstream, Simone went onto develop a captivating voice of force, of deep and intense emotion, that shone through her powerfully moving poetics and performance.

While writing this book and reflecting upon my own experiences, as well as the experiences of my participants, I found so much solace in Simone; her journey helped me to navigate feelings of being under-valued, dismissed, and low self-worth. What made me smile and never allowed my spirit to break lay in the simple fact that the joke was on Curtis, not Simone. Simone apparently just didn't 'make the cut' for Curtis, but more fool them, because she went onto be one of the most influential artists of all time. Of course, Curtis and various commentators were quick to deny racism, allegedly they just had a very high standard which on the day Simone apparently failed to meet—besides it couldn't have been racism because Curtis had previously accepted African American male pianists. Similarly, when they don't offer us the job, or fail to promote us, we are assured it's not because of racism, but rather because we just failed to meet the specific criteria—besides it couldn't have been racism because the department previously employed a male academic of colour. It is precisely this empty rhetoric that allows white institutions to simultaneously legitimize their insidious practices of racism by delegitimizing our realities of racism. It is important therefore that we, as racially marked academics, never forget that we did not fail, but rather the institution failed us.

In another interview Simone said:

> I sing from intelligence. I sing from letting them know that I know who they are, and what they have done to my people around the world. That's not anger- anger has its place, and fire moves things. But I sing from intelligence. (Simone 1999, March 25)

Racially marked academics know all too well what it feels like to be rejected and excluded conceptually by the 'canon' of our disciplines, and in actuality through the broader racist structures of our institutions. We are viewed most of the time as angry, polemical and antagonistic. However, if we take the experiences of Nina Simone seriously, we can see that being on the margins is also to occupy a space of renewed intellect, creativity and a voice of resistance. And here again, we must return to hooks in remembering marginality 'as a site one stays in, clings to even because it nourishes one's capacity to resist. It offers to one the possibility of radical perspective from which to see and create, to imagine alternatives, new worlds' (1989: 20). Simone's jazz, gospel, soul, and protest songs made more of an impact on music and politics than those in the mainstream could ever have hoped to achieve. She remains a cultural symbol for black experiences, and her iconography continues to be celebrated and revered as she clearly demonstrated that out of rejection arose an artistic, critical and electrifying political voice that not only spoke to people of colour, but also engaged the majority by holding up a mirror to illuminate their brutal practices of racial oppression.

Simone once said that she was too old to keep asking for love from the industry.[4] Perhaps we, as racially marked academics, need to also stop seeking love, acceptance, and validation from our white institutions, and instead focus on cultivating our collective bonds to develop a strong voice that supports and uplifts not only each other, but also our communities. We may be on the margins of the academy and of society, but collaboratively we can perhaps navigate more effectively our shared struggles and at the very least fracture the structures of power and privilege that have overshadowed our experiences for too long; like Simone we too must find the strength to be real rebels with a cause.

Notes

1. This argument originally appeared in the following online article: Sian, K. (2017, March 14) '"We're Drawing the Line": Our Fight Against University Marketization Is About More Than Pensions,' *Ceasefire Magazine*, UK. https://ceasefiremagazine.co.uk/were-drawing-line-fight-university-marketization-pensions/#commenting.
2. Examples of such earlier literature were mapped out in the introduction to this book.
3. Recent literature includes: Gabriel, D., and Tate, S. (2017) *Inside the Ivory Tower: Black British Academics*, London: Trentham Books; Ahmed, S. (2012) *On Being Included: Racism and Diversity in*

Institutional Life, Durham: Duke University Press; Bhambra, G., Gebrial, D., and Nişancıoğlu, K. (2018) *Decolonizing the University*, London: Pluto; Arday, J., and Mirza, H. (2018) *Dismantling Race in Higher Education: Racism, Whiteness and Decolonising the Academy*, London: Palgrave.
4. Simone, N. (1984, March 14) Interview by Mavis Nicholson. '*Afternoon with Mavis Nicholson*,' broadcasted on UK TV Channel 4.

References

Gillborn, D. (2013). Interest-Divergence and the Colour of Cutbacks: Race, Recession and the Undeclared War on Black Children. *Discourse: Studies in the Cultural Politics of Education, 34*(4), 477–491.

hooks, b. (1989). Choosing the Margin as a Space of Racial Openness. *The Journal of Cinema and Media, 36*, 15–23.

Light, A. (2017). *What Happened, Miss Simone?* Edinburgh: Canongate Books Ltd.

Sian, K. (2017, March 14). "We're Drawing the Line": Our Fight Against University Marketization Is About More Than Pensions. *Ceasefire Magazine*. https://ceasefiremagazine.co.uk/were-drawing-line-fight-university-marketization-pensions/#commenting.

Simone, N. (1999, March 25). Interview by Tim Sebastian. '*Hard Talk*,' broadcasted on BBC.

Simone, N. (2003). *I Put a Spell on You: The Autobiography of Nina Simone* (2nd ed.). Cambridge, MA: DaCapo Press.

Index

© The Editor(s) (if applicable) and The Author(s) 2019
K. P. Sian, *Navigating Institutional Racism in British Universities*,
Mapping Global Racisms, https://doi.org/10.1007/978-3-030-14284-1

Printed by Printforce, the Netherlands